WEALTH
Your Way

A SIMPLE PATH TO
FINANCIAL FREEDOM

Cosmo P. DeStefano

HOUNDSTOOTH
PRESS

WEALTH YOUR WAY
A Simple Path to Financial Freedom

ISBN   978-1-5445-2983-7   *Hardcover*

        978-1-5445-2984-4   *Paperback*

        978-1-5445-2985-1   *Ebook*

CONTENTS

To Zach and Nadia. Find joy in life's journey
knowing you are unique and loved unconditionally.

For my wife, Tina. With great wisdom
I asked her the question, and with my greater luck,
she accepted my proposal of marriage.

INTRODUCTION

BEFORE RETIRING FROM MY PROFESSIONAL CAREER AS A CERTIFIED public accountant (CPA) and tax consultant, I spent 22 years as a partner in a so-called "Big Four" public accounting firm (one of the largest professional services firms in the world with a global network of more than 284,000 people across 155 countries). I worked with clients big and small, public and private, across various industries helping them solve some of their more complex business and financial issues.

So it came as a bit of a surprise to me when I realized that one of my toughest financial challenges wasn't in the professional realm, but rather at home, teaching my two children about money matters, among life's other lessons. It wasn't the teaching that was the problem, it was the learning—or at least that's what I tell myself! Both caught on quickly enough about the importance of money (most kids do), but neither of them had much interest in spending time delving into broader financial matters or "boring business stuff" as they would often say. I don't blame them—few people get as juiced up about personal financial planning as I do.

As the years went by, the conversations kept broadening out, first to several nieces and nephews, then to business associates, friends, and neighbors. I started summarizing my thoughts in a monthly email, each covering a different aspect of personal finance. The distribution and forwarding of those emails, which started with just a few family members, struck a chord and quickly expanded. Shortly thereafter, several readers suggested I put my thoughts all in one place.

This book has grown out of my efforts to teach financial matters to my children, who have their own interests and passions to follow. My simple wish for them is that they learn how planning for money matters can enhance their personal life's journey, and maybe the lessons in this book can also help them avoid a few missteps along the way. And since you are reading this book, I hope it can do the same for you.

Company pensions are for the most part a thing of the past. Social Security was designed to supplement your retirement income, but it was never intended to be your sole source of retirement spending money. Today, managing your money is not an option but an imperative. On your own or with the help of an advisor, you need to do it.

This book and my philosophy on planning personal wealth management are based on the concept that *accumulating wealth is simple but not easy*. If it's simple, why does it take a whole book to explain it? It doesn't. I can summarize the concept in one (long) sentence: define what financial independence (FI) means for you, set realistic goals, develop a plan to achieve those goals with the right balance of risk and return, periodically review your progress, make changes as needed, and stay on your chosen path over the several decades that make up your Life's Complete Financial Arc.

Simple, right? So, why this book? It takes more than a sentence (1) to flush out all that is packed into that summation, and (2) to identify and explore ways to deal with the pitfalls and hurdles that can make the journey "not easy."

To start, we will step back and explore what we are planning for in the first place—that is, what is "wealth" and "financial independence"? We will explore how to develop a dynamic planning process, set realistic goals and assess progress toward those goals, identify some challenges, and, yes, explore some investing strategies including this fundamental understanding: investing is an important tool to help achieve your plan, but investing is not *the* plan. And the plan is not as critical as the planning process!

We will also delve into some of the philosophy and psychology of wealth planning, helping you recognize your cognitive biases and the emotional challenges hurled at you by market participants and pundits.

All these concepts come under the umbrella of financial independence: How to think more broadly and holistically about your money plans. How to get to the point that you no longer need your labor to generate income to live on. How to grow your wealth and achieve the freedom of financial independence—the freedom to continue exploring the interests that provide you meaning and purpose in life.

In a lot of ways, the journey to FI is like dieting or exercising. Eating right or working out is simple enough. But it's the design and execution of the plan that can be daunting. Dragging yourself to the gym when you don't feel like going. Eating a salad for dinner when you just want to tie on the feed bag. Both diet and exercise are simple concepts but both take time, discipline, and patience to see lasting results.

The same is true with planning to grow your wealth. Financial independence is not simple because, as Warren Buffett once said, "Nobody wants to get rich slow." What do successful weight watchers, exercisers, and FI-ers have in common? They all like and want to achieve their goals. They find motivation in the end result, which drives them forward throughout their journey's ups and downs. They are truly comforted by working toward their goals. We will examine ways to find comfort with our financial journey.

Our plan will traverse your Life's Complete Financial Arc. It's much broader than "investing" just as sustainable weight loss encompasses more than "eating less." We will discuss a planning process to accumulate wealth, achieve the pinnacle of financial independence, and then withdraw that wealth every month for as long as you live. A planning process that is simple and *easier* to execute.

As Sy Syms (Founder of the Syms discount clothing retailer) said in his first TV commercial in 1974 and repeated for 37 years, "An educated consumer is our best customer." That's why my goal here is to help you with *how* to think about personal financial planning, not just *what* to think.

Retirement is a date: one moment in time. But it also describes an extended period: the decades-long phase of life after you "graduate" from work. We want to focus less on the date and more on the decades of enjoyment.

Early in my career on a random Tuesday afternoon, my friend Chuck and I were in the back of the elevator heading down to lunch. Bob, an older gentleman and a seasoned professional whom we both admired, was by the doors with his back to us. Chuck and I were working a lot of hours, talking about how long the week already felt and how it seemed like it would just drag on. Both of us agreed we couldn't wait for Friday to get here. At that moment, the doors opened to the fifth floor. Bob stepped out, turned around, and as the doors were closing quietly said, "Don't wish your life away, boys."

I didn't know it at the time, but Bob's one line of advice was the seed that grew into something much bigger: my eventual realization that rather than hoping and wishing about the future, I'd be much better off planning my path to a future of my choosing (and that's much broader than just finances).

When it comes to money, having a robust financial planning process makes it easier to enjoy the near term, living your best life without wishing for tomorrow to hurry up and arrive. Why? Because you have peace of mind that your long-term plans are on course. And if you drift off the path, you will have the confidence to make necessary course corrections.

Investing is a tool to execute your plan. Without a plan, investing becomes a flurry of activity with no clear direction: a nebulous journey devoid of well-defined personal goals. You need an overarching financial planning process and financial goals on which your investment portfolio strives to deliver. Investing to "make bank" is not a holistic financial plan!

This book is dedicated to helping you level set your core understanding of financial independence and develop default behaviors that are well suited to help you plan for and achieve your financial goals while living and enjoying your best life now.

You may be a Gen Z coming of age, or a millennial with oppressive student debt, or a boomer playing catch-up, but for all of us financial planning boils down to this simple mantra: think about what to do, go do it, then do as little as possible after that! PCR: Plan, Course-Correct, Repeat.

DISCLAIMER

THIS BOOK IS FOR EDUCATIONAL PURPOSES ONLY. IT IS NOT INTENDED to be nor should it be construed as legal, tax, investment, financial, or other advice. This book covers broad topics for a wide audience. It is not individualized guidance tailored to any one person. It is up to you to own your decisions and to seek out a competent professional should you need expert advice regarding your personal circumstances.

This book is a summation of my personal experiences (the good, the bad, and the ugly) over 35 years of planning, investing, reaching financial independence, and now enjoying the freedom my retirement years are providing me.

It is based on what has worked (and is working) for me, and references several other books and studies that have resonated with me as I developed my opinions on accumulating and spending wealth. This book is in no way intended to be an exhaustive study of such literature or any of the topics discussed herein. You should use this book as one component of your self-education on personal financial matters and financial independence.

To assist you with your continuing education, I have included at the end of each chapter suggestions for additional reading. (Some books are referenced more than once since they cover multiple topics.)

1

WHERE ARE YOU GOING?

"If you fail to plan, you are planning to fail."

—BENJAMIN FRANKLIN

OVER THE YEARS, THE FIRST FINANCIAL QUESTION A LOT OF PEOPLE ask me has remained remarkably consistent: *"Where should I invest my money?"* Everyone is eager to jump right into investing. Eager but often equally scared to act. To combat the inertia and leverage that eagerness, my response has been as consistent: to start, invest in low-cost, broad-based index funds for the core of your financial independence (FI) Portfolio[1]—for example, the Vanguard Total Stock Market Index ETF, ticker symbol "VTI." (More on this topic later.) It's that simple. Get started.

Now that we have this burning question out of the way, I encourage you to pause and take a deep breath. Step back for a moment and reflect on this: *"Where should I invest my money?"* is a good question, but it arguably should not be your first question and it definitely shouldn't be your only one! Investing is critical, but "why" and "how" should come before "where," or at least be addressed concurrently. If we invest without purpose (the "why") and without a plan (the "how"), then famed New York Yankee Yogi Berra said it best: "We're lost but we're making good time!"

As we get on the path to financial freedom, we will explore throughout this book the "why" and "how" of investing, which will also help us address the "where." If you understand "why" and "how," then developing your personalized plan and staying on your path becomes less scary and a lot more manageable.

We are not investing simply to try and "make bank." We need specific goals for our wealth accumulation and a plan to achieve those goals. As we will discuss in more detail, investing is not a financial plan, but just one of many tools to help execute your plan.

Goals give you a sense of direction. Without goals and a plan, investors merely react to short-term events without considering the long-term ramifications. A plan keeps you focused on your targeted results and keeps you motivated to work toward those goals. Just like with dieting and exercising, envisioning the joy in the end result is a powerful motivator. In other words, your financial plan needs to be purpose-built and goals-driven.

Investing to "make a pot of money" is not a goal. It's not specific. As an example, a better-defined goal might be something like: *"I want to retire by age 58 with $80,000 of annual cash flow to meet my $75,000 of calculated spending needs and provide $5,000 of cushion for unforeseen expenses."* This is the kind of goal we can plan for and attain.

And most importantly, a well-thought-out plan will provide processes and guidelines for making current and future decisions, especially when faced with unforeseen and inevitable changes that will pop up over a multidecade time frame. A good planning process encourages rigor around contingencies. It helps you adapt to previously unknown events as they unfold—the kind of stuff that blindsides you on some random afternoon. No one-and-done plan can accomplish that.

More broadly, we need a holistic financial planning process. In designing our process, we can frame our thoughts by addressing three simple questions:

1. *What do I have?* (an accurate accounting of what is in your FI Portfolio today)

2. *What do I want?* (retirement monthly cash needs and for how long)

3. *How do I get what I want?* (planning to bridge the gap between 1 and 2)

Take inventory, define your goals, and create a plan to achieve those goals, adjusting as you go. PCR: Plan, Course-Correct, Repeat.

INVESTING IS A TOOL, NOT A PLAN

Once you start mapping out the answer to question three and charting your course, you will see that there are multiple variables that you need to think about in addition to investing. For example, how much money will you contribute to the plan each month and for how many years; what are your retirement spending goals and are they flexible; how many years will you be working; will you have other sources of income (e.g., Social Security or a pension); are you planning to leave a bequest; do you want to spend down your portfolio or live on only the income it generates, etc.

Specific investment selections will flow from this planning process as a key component of the plan, but by no means is investing the entire plan. Remember, charting a course to achieve your financial goals is the plan. Fully exploring all the possible answers to *"Where should I invest my money?"* comes toward the *end* of this planning process, not the beginning.

> **NOTE:** As we will learn in the next chapter, your monthly contributions will be more impactful to your wealth accumulation than will the rate of return on your investments. Therefore, getting started with saving and investing as soon as possible is critically important even if you don't have a fully baked plan just yet!

So, where do we start? With the end in mind. By first defining our ultimate financial goal.

In designing your plan, you need well-defined, specific goals. Let's start by coming up with a simple and clear definition of our ultimate, overarching goal. Is it to retire? Invest in stocks or real estate? Get out of debt? Beat the market? Travel the world? Leave a legacy? The short answer: nope. None of these is the ultimate goal but each of these could be included in the journey. These all could be buoys, landmarks, and ports of call along the way of your financial voyage but they are not the ultimate destination.

Think higher level. The ultimate money goal we all are (or should be) sailing toward is financial independence. Don't worry, we'll make this a better-defined goal with numbers later on.

Financial independence means you have accumulated enough wealth so that all your future financial needs can be paid for from your FI Portfolio without needing your labor to earn a salary. You no longer *need* to work although you may *choose* to work for other than financial reasons.

> *"Money frees you from doing things you dislike. Since I dislike doing nearly everything, money is handy."*
> —GROUCHO MARX

Simply stated, your FI Portfolio buys you the most desirable asset on the planet—freedom. Freedom to spend your money, and more importantly your time, as you see fit. Freedom to choose to retire (or not), volunteer, travel the world, be philanthropic, spend more time with family and friends, build a legacy, etc. In other words, freedom to more fully explore and dive into your core personal interests—those interests that bring you the most joy and fulfillment. Financial independence is not just a number—it is a state of mind. It provides freedom in a broad sense, and isn't that what we all ultimately desire?

NOTE: A point of clarity. Don't confuse financial independence with being "rich." How do you know if you are rich? The only way to tell is to compare yourself to others. "Rich" is a relative term. You are rich if you have more (how much more?) than others around you. If you ask 10 people to define "rich," I'm willing to bet you'd get 10 different answers. "Rich" may be a fun topic to debate over drinks with friends, but it will produce no meaningful intel (and may produce some nagging resentment!). Financial independence, on the other hand, is more specific, more personal. You have enough money **for you**, regardless of how your portfolio balance compares to others. Financial independence is freedom, defined one person at a time.

"If you don't change direction, you may end up where you are heading."

—**LAO TZU**

Knowing your destination makes creating a plan and charting a course to get there a whole lot easier. Financial independence is the ultimate goal and it is going to require planning, time, money, and a little wind at our backs. In the meantime, however, you need to live your life, and that also costs money.

To reconcile the push and pull of current versus future (retirement) spending, you need to come to terms with two simple and undeniable truths: (1) You cannot save any money if you spend all your income; and (2) You cannot save all your income because you need to spend money to live.

YOU CANNOT INVEST IF YOU DON'T FIRST SAVE CASH

The journey to FI, therefore, requires that you gain control of your income and current spending so that you can plan for tomorrow while enjoying today. Before you start investing for the future, you need to first identify and quantify the cash you have available to save.

So, at the highest level, your first step in your planning process is to split your income into a few manageable spending categories or buckets. I suggest four buckets to start. Bucket A is for long-term investing, building your FI Portfolio. Buckets B, C, and D are for everything else! Simple enough?

Here is an example of a four-bucket approach:

Get Control of Your Income and Expenses Guidelines for Spending (adjust to personal preference)		
bucket A	**FI Portfolio** [401(k), Roth IRA, brokerage account, CDs, real estate, etc.]	10–15%
bucket B	**Fixed Living Costs** [taxes, housing, groceries, debt, clothing, etc.]	55–70%
bucket C	**Saving Goals** [vacations, house down payment, emergency cash for unexpected expenses]	5–15%
bucket D	**Spending on Whatever** [dining out, entertainment, and anything else!]	15–20%

The sum of what you allocate to each of the four buckets should equal 100% of your income. That way, you know you have accounted for all your sources of cash.

> **NOTE:** Don't get hung up on where to invest Bucket A. As we said at the beginning of this chapter, pick a low-cost, broad-based index fund and just get started. At this stage, investment selection is not nearly as important as the focus on saving cash every month. **Be a saver first, then move on to being an investor.**

The more detailed you get within each of these buckets, the better off you will be. Understanding all the cash that is coming in and the details of where that cash is currently being spent will help you uncover opportunities to reallocate among the buckets. For example, a category you label as "miscellaneous" that adds up to 20% of your income likely warrants a more detailed analysis!

> **NOTE:** Don't get carried away chasing down every $10 purchase. This is an iterative process. Make the first pass at the buckets. You can (and will) revisit your bucket allocations later. Just get started.

To be clear, this *is not* about you cutting out your morning five-dollar latte because it adds up to "a lot" of money over the course of a year. It *is* about becoming more aware of where you choose to spend your money—and understanding the financial implications of the choices you make.

MANY PEOPLE OBSESS ABOUT EARNING MONEY, BUT WHAT THEY SHOULD OBSESS ABOUT IS HOW TO USE MONEY

The allocation percentages in the table are just a reference point. How you spend your money is up to you. For example, some people with student loans or other debt, heavy housing costs, and high taxes may need up to 70% in Bucket B. Others (e.g., who have finished paying off their debt) may find 55–70% is much too high and can immediately redirect cash elsewhere (preferably to their FI Portfolio).

I would also suggest that as the years pass and you progress in your career, your preferences and willingness/affordability to move between buckets will also change. Personal choices all along the way.

Buckets B–D cover all your monthly living expenses. They also include costs that may be a few years out such as buying a new car or saving for a house, a tropical vacation, etc.—every expense that someday your FI Portfolio will cover but for the near term you need to fund from other sources, mainly wages from your labor. Buckets B–D are what you will live on until Bucket A, your FI Portfolio, is large enough to support you in the lifestyle of your choosing.

YOUR WORKING INCOME WILL FUND YOUR CURRENT SPENDING, BUT IT'S YOUR FI PORTFOLIO THAT WILL FUND YOUR FINANCIAL FREEDOM

Buckets B–D provide everyday cash, but here is the key. Every month you need to contribute to Bucket A *before* Buckets B–D. Start with your gross income. Decide what you want to contribute to your FI Portfolio, say, for example, 10%. The rest can then be spread among Buckets B, C, and D.

Make it an iterative process. If 10% into Bucket A leaves you with too much in Buckets B–D, then consider starting Bucket A at greater than 10%. The key is to just get started and stay *consistent* with monthly contributions to Bucket A. This is a big step in the right direction, and coupled with persistence, the right start rarely finishes in the wrong place.

Contributing to Bucket A goes by a few memorable monikers—"Pay yourself first," "Live below your means," "Take it off the top," "Spend less than you earn"—but understanding the rationale (the "why") for Bucket A coming first is critical: you are enabling time and the power of compounding (which we will discuss in Chapter Three) to do their thing. Even if you spend every last dollar in Buckets B–D, you will always have Bucket A working for your financial future.

Alternatively, you could spend your income first and then at the end of each month try to find some cash to save, but often life gets in the way and there is nothing left to add to Bucket A. That would be a giant mistake.

As we will learn more in later chapters, a **consistent** monthly contribution is the single largest factor in growing your wealth. So, listen to Warren Buffett, the Oracle of Omaha: "Don't save what's left after spending. Spend what's left after saving."

GET TO THE GYM AND EAT RIGHT

I know individuals who have earned large sums of money over their careers as they honed their craft to be among the best in their chosen profession. As they now contemplate the cost of retiring, they wonder aloud why they never found any measure of wealth. Here is the simple answer: *they never sought it.* Knowing what to do and doing it are not the same thing. Financial independence won't just happen to you. Just like going to the gym or eating healthier, you need to more than just want it—you need to go do it.

> **NOTE:** High income is not wealth. If you make a lot of money and spend a lot of money you have no wealth. Income is what you make from working. Wealth is what you keep and add to your FI Portfolio. Income is not wealth, but assets that generate income are wealth. Keep accumulating those assets and growing your FI Portfolio.

DON'T CONFUSE "SAVING" WITH "SAVINGS"

When you bargain shop and find the item you want for a lower price or you decide to not make a purchase altogether, you are saving money. Simply put, less money is leaving your wallet. While the avoidance of an expenditure is saving money, the cash is still in your wallet available to be spent another day. And in so doing, you have merely substituted today's expense for one tomorrow. "Saving" probably makes you feel good (who doesn't like a bargain?!), but it doesn't grow your FI Portfolio, which is where your "savings" reside.

A while back I was speaking with a couple who sat down at the kitchen table and made a list of all the money they had saved over a two-decade marriage with do-it-yourself home improvement projects. Being very handy, both had tackled carpentry (including a small house addition), masonry, landscaping, and painting projects. In their estimation, what they saved totaled more than $100,000. Very impressive.

They sat back quite happy with themselves, and unseeingly content with approximately zero dollars in their FI Portfolio and mortgage debt that had grown to twice the size of what it was a decade prior.

Saving money is a good first step, but what matters in our FI journey is what we do with the saved cash. I'm not saying that spending it elsewhere is bad, but don't be lulled into thinking that "saving" on an expense automatically increases your wealth.

"Saving is not savings" is the corollary to the concept that "income is not wealth." Building your savings (your wealth) happens when you add to your FI Portfolio, not when you bargain shop and save 30% on clothes only to use the saved dollars to buy shoes to go with your new outfit.

"I always say, complacency is the kiss of death."

—SHARI REDSTONE

Whatever your bucket allocations are, don't become complacent. For example, if you are currently putting 10% into Bucket A, don't stay satisfied for long. You should be thinking about ways to get to 11%. And when you get to 11% then target 12%, and so on. This means you are looking for ways to allocate more of your gross income to Bucket A and less elsewhere. A good place to start is with a salary increase or bonus. Where will all that new cash go?

Some of the more successful FI Portfolio builders I know are putting 20%, 30%, even 40%+ of their income toward their portfolio, especially later in their careers (or early in their careers if they are living with their parents!). Ten percent contributed to your FI Portfolio might be where lots of people start, but it's not where the most successful FI planners finish.

"Chains of habit are too light to be felt until they are too heavy to be broken."

—WARREN BUFFETT

You also need to automate the process. Set up automatic monthly contributions to your FI accounts. Set up automatic monthly payments for your credit card and other bills so you never carry a balance and incur finance charges. No thinking about it. No remembering to move cash at the end of every month. It just happens—automatically.

Allow good habits to dominate your mind and actions so that negative habits do not have the chance to take hold. In other words, develop good financial habits and make them stick. This will supercharge your wealth accumulation and grow your FI Portfolio. Do not get weighed down with bad habits!

> *"We don't have a trillion-dollar debt because we haven't taxed enough; we have a trillion-dollar debt because we spend too much."*
>
> **—RONALD REAGAN**

A lot of people tell me they want to get out of debt sooner rather than later, a choice I strongly support. They then ask if they should pay off debt before investing in their future. In effect, they are asking if they should take from Bucket A to put toward an item in Bucket B. If you look at the four buckets we just discussed, you might see why I think that's too narrow a question.

People love binary choices: Coke or Pepsi? Disney World or Universal? FI or debt? But sometimes you need to step back and think a little broader. Bucket A isn't the only potential source of extra cash to go toward paying off the debt early. Any combination of the four buckets (including from within Bucket B) could provide more cash to pay down debt, potentially without sacrificing any of your FI Portfolio contribution.

Let's say you start with 10% of your income going into Bucket A. If you decide to pay more than the minimum monthly payment on your debt (again, I would applaud this decision), then it's up to you where the extra cash comes from—either the 10% that you're putting into your FI Portfolio or the 90% you're spending on every-thing else. (How about that binary choice?)

> **NOTE:** No matter which bucket(s) you ultimately take the extra cash from, once the debt is finally paid off, I would suggest that the monthly cash you were using to pay the debt (or at least a very large percentage of it) should get redirected into your FI Portfolio.

Your choices aren't always about the money, but you should understand the financial implications of the choices you make—preferably before you make them.

WHEN SAVING AND SPENDING BRING YOU EQUAL HAPPINESS, YOU ARE WELL ON YOUR WAY

Once you have a firm grasp on Bucket A *and* your FI plan, then enjoy your spending! The ancillary benefit of executing a well-thought-out FI planning process is that you can feel good, not guilty, about spending what's left in Buckets B–D. I'm not suggest-ing you become a spendthrift, but don't become a miser either. It's about finding the right balance—planning for tomorrow while also enjoying today.

I remember seeing a Dilbert comic strip in which Wally tells his boss he saved enough money to retire and wonders aloud why no one has come up with a name for that amount of cash. Wally's boss responds with a resounding FU!

Like Wally, we are all striving to have "enough" money in our FI Portfolio. (Wally might call it his FU Portfolio.) Patience and discipline will lead you there.

In the 2014 movie *The Gambler*, a loan shark named Frank (played by actor John Goodman) expounds on Wally's concept of FU money to gambler Jim Bennett (played by Mark Wahlberg). In a powerful scene Frank explains, with rather colorful language, that Jim should rechannel his "FU" attitude toward life into developing the liberating freedom that "FU money" can provide.

My description does not do justice to the acting talent of John Goodman. Here is a QR-code link to a YouTube video of the scene I am referring to.[2]

Don't dwell on the $2.5 million they discuss. That's Frank's number (you'll calculate your number in due course). And while I do not advocate gambling to reach your goal, look past the indelicate language and focus on the moral of the story—reach financial independence and you will have freedom.

NOTE: Those of you with a little more experience might recall the precursor to FU money, the KMA Club. Anecdotally, the club originated in the government sector. As employees logged the requisite number of working years and became fully vested in their maximum pension, they joyfully declared themselves members of the Kiss My Ass Club.

I can say with certainty that you will achieve financial independence on one of two days: the day you die or someday sooner. The choice is yours.

SUGGESTIONS FOR ADDITIONAL READING

J. L. Collins, *The Simple Path to Wealth: Your Road Map to Financial Independence and a Rich, Free Life* (CreateSpace Publishing, 2016).

Wes Moss, *You Can Retire Sooner than You Think: The 5 Money Secrets of the Happiest Retirees* (McGraw-Hill, 2014).

Carl Richards, *The One-Page Financial Plan: A Simple Way to Be Smart about Your Money* (Penguin Publishing Group, 2015).

Thomas J. Stanley and William D. Danko, *The Millionaire Next Door: The Surprising Secrets of America's Wealthy* (Longstreet Press, 1996).

2

CHARTING YOUR COURSE

"You cannot escape the responsibility of tomorrow by evading it today."

—ABRAHAM LINCOLN

"*WHAT'S YOUR NUMBER?*" IF YOU EVER HAVE MORE THAN A CASUAL FI conversation with friends or acquaintances, one of you is very likely to ask or be asked the somewhat intrusive question, "*What's your number?*" The questioner is trying to assess the total FI Portfolio balance needed to achieve financial independence. As we've discussed, the answer is individual-specific, but that doesn't stop the inquisitiveness. Twenty-five years ago, I asked the question of a friend, call him Billy Bob, and the response was "$2.5 to $3 million." Years later, toward the end of Billy's very successful career, I again asked the question, and this time Billy Bob responded, "$12,000." Huh?

You will spend your entire career accumulating wealth to get to your number. And someday along the way, hopefully no later than today, you are going to come to the critical realization that getting to your number (i.e., the desired total balance in your portfolio) is only halfway on your FI journey. You then need to take withdrawals from your FI Portfolio to meet your spending needs for the remainder of your life. Billy Bob realized that having a $3 million portfolio is all well and good, but it's ultimately the monthly cash withdrawals that will pay for his living expenses. And how much can be safely withdrawn without running out?

Just as you plan your monthly contributions, you need to project and plan those withdrawals. You will build your FI Portfolio monthly and then you will withdraw from it monthly. Those withdrawals will be your version of Billy Bob's $12,000 *per month*.

> *"Liberty means responsibility. That is why most men dread it."*
> —GEORGE BERNARD SHAW

There are two basic ways to approach planning and managing your FI Portfolio. On one hand, you can simply start investing, hopefully accumulating wealth for a bunch of years until one day you proclaim, "I have enough and I've had enough!" You then quit your job and start withdrawing every month, hoping the money doesn't expire before you do. (Can you hear Doris Day singing "Que Sera, Sera"?) I'm not sure about you, but this approach would most certainly leave me with some sleepless nights.

On the other hand, you can start investing while also projecting out what your FI Portfolio balance might look like on your FI date.

You then take the additional step of projecting how to withdraw a monthly amount and how long those withdrawals might last. You effectively map out your projected cash flows over your entire life (both the accumulation and the withdrawal stages)— your Life's Complete Financial Arc. What is the biggest advantage of doing this full lifecycle analysis now over the "whatever" approach? If you don't like the projected answers, you have time to course-correct.

We know our ultimate goal is financial independence, meaning your FI Portfolio can provide you an acceptable monthly cash flow that you don't outlive. To get there, we know we're going to accumulate wealth in our FI Portfolio. But how do you monitor the progress of your wealth accumulation plan and how do you know *when* you have enough (your FI date) to generate those monthly withdrawals so you can consider leaving the workforce, traveling the world, etc.?

As we said earlier, the best place to start is with your end goals in mind and designing a plan to get there. Create a holistic, full lifecycle plan that covers your cash flows during *both* the accumulation stage and the withdrawal stage—Life's Complete Financial Arc.

Design your plan so that, at a minimum, your FI Portfolio provides enough monthly cash flow to cover all your living expenses starting on your FI date and continuing for the rest of your life.

A plan is both a process and a reference point to periodically measure progress. To some, all this planning stuff sounds like a tall order. Let's break it down and use some tools to do the heavy lifting.

> *"Whether you think you can or think you can't, you are right."*
>
> **—HENRY FORD**

I purposefully think in terms of nautical charts—not roadmaps—when describing the voyage to and through financial independence. Unlike roadmaps, nautical charts do not always show a predetermined path. Rather, it's up to the navigator to plot or course-correct using current data and navigational aids.

Just as the ocean's tides and depths change, so too do the financial markets and economic realities. Once you set your financial plan in motion, you and your plan need to be flexible and you must adapt to the changing conditions. Take in new information, talk with people whose wisdom you trust, and reevaluate. It's a living, breathing process. How you choose to navigate the ever-changing financial "ocean," including emotionally, will be critically important.

AT SOME POINT, REACHING YOUR DESTINATION WILL REQUIRE CHANGING YOUR DIRECTION

If you are off just one degree in a spaceship leaving the moon and returning to Cape Canaveral, you would be off course by about one mile in the first minute. A simple course correction since you have 238,000 more miles to travel. But what would happen if you failed to course-correct for that one small degree? Well, I hope you packed a bathing suit. By the time you traveled those 238,000 miles, you would miss Florida by more than 4,000 miles, arriving west of Los Angeles some 1,500 miles out in the middle of the Pacific Ocean. A one-degree course correction combined with time leads to big changes.

The true benefit of financial planning is not only to envision the endgame but, more importantly, to link the accumulation stage and the withdrawal stage into one unified plan. A plan that provides a process to deal with the unforeseen circumstances and erroneous assumptions that inevitably reveal themselves as time goes by. Course corrections.

Consider the plan a snapshot of your progress toward your FI goals. The process of mapping, planning, reevaluating, and course-correcting is an exercise in financial awareness. Studies show that people who follow an FI plan are more successful than those who don't.

WHICH DAY OF THE WEEK IS "SOMEDAY"?

Ready to get started? There are several "free" retirement calculators online—do a Google search. Some of the online calculators are linked to advisors and their services where getting the detailed output you seek is tied to signing up (not quite my definition of "free"). There are also a few very good online calculators that come without catches and that do a decent job of running projections for you. The best of these calculators cover both the wealth accumulation stage and the withdrawal stage: Life's Complete Financial Arc. Working with online calculators is a good way to begin to get your head around a broad view of your plan. You can always decide to pay for more intensive and detailed projections, but I suggest you start with a top-down simplified model.

I would also suggest you use two or three different models since they all have different limitations. With so many personal variables (timeline, rates of return, contributions, withdrawals, inflation, etc.), it's extremely hard for any one calculator to be your panacea for modeling.

To start you off, one online calculator I've found to be detailed enough without being overly cumbersome to navigate can be found at financial-calculators.com/retirement-calculator.[3] To be clear, this website does offer products for sale, but this calculator is currently fully functional without making a purchase or signing up for anything. (I have no affiliation with this site.)

I like their graphic output because it shows in one picture an estimate of your Life's Complete Financial Arc: accumulating wealth, "Pre-Retirement Investing" (green bars); hitting your FI date; and then the withdrawal stage, "Post Retirement Income" (red bars), as you live your FI lifestyle. Don't be intimidated. Just put in some assumptions and play around with it.

The more you use it, the more comfortable you will become with the modeling exercise. This is just one example of a model; there are many out there. Traditional fund managers such as Vanguard, Ameriprise, Fidelity, and Schwab offer online retirement calculators. Most financial advisors also have access to third-party or proprietary models.

If you are using money management software, you may already have access to a modeling calculator. For example, I use Quicken software and it contains a tool they call the Lifetime Planner. While I use Quicken primarily to manage my day-to-day finances, the Lifetime Planner is a convenient way for me to periodically monitor and course-correct my Life's Complete Financial Arc.

Whether you use a website, an app, or software, or work with an advisor, you need to get your data organized and summarized in one place. To effectively manage your FI Portfolio and populate a model, you first need to accurately measure the data. Garbage in, garbage out.

> **NOTE:** Retirement calculators give you a glimpse into **a** future, but not necessarily **the** future. With so many variables and a decades-long unknowable future, precision is an impractical goal. Use the output from calculators and models as directional indicators, not precise destinations.

CONGRESS MAY HAVE ACTUALLY DONE SOMETHING PRODUCTIVE

I am not the only one who thinks you should be doing this modeling regularly. The SECURE Act (Setting Every Community Up for Retirement Enhancement) was signed into law by President Trump in late December 2019. In part, it requires plan sponsors to annually disclose on 401(k) statements an estimate of the monthly payments participants would receive if their total account balance were used to purchase an annuity for the participant and the participant's surviving spouse. In other words, the disclosure will translate the total balance into an estimate of what the participant might receive in monthly payments over their remaining lifetime.

The law directs the Secretary of Labor to develop baseline assumptions and a model disclosure.

Congress is trying to help you think about FI in terms of monthly cash flow (which is a mind-shift for a lot of folks who have spent decades focused on simply getting to as big a number as possible). And since you are a fastidious wealth accumulator, your 401(k) is only one piece of your broader FI Portfolio. Doing your own modeling means you can include your entire FI Portfolio (401[k], savings and brokerage accounts, IRAs, real estate, etc.) and tailor the model to your unique circumstances.

BE PROACTIVE AND PROSPECTIVE

I find myself reviewing financial results and goals at the close of each year. I do it in January for no other reason than the calendar year just feels like a natural (albeit arbitrary) cutoff. And just like spending time over the holidays reminiscing with family and friends, I also find myself reflecting on my financial year that has just ended.

My thoughts run the gamut: *I wish I had saved more each month; I celebrate almost beating the market; I wish I had bought AMD/Amazon/ Netflix ten years ago; I should have shorted Kraft Heinz/Macy's/PG&E before they collapsed*, etc., etc., etc. All kinds of backward-looking, capricious thoughts. Most of this retrospection is not very fruitful. So, whether you are lamenting the fact that you didn't do better or celebrating your brilliance, keep it brief and get on with it. Leave the past in the past. All that matters now is the balance in your FI Portfolio today, and where it's going tomorrow. Is your FI plan still on course to get you where you want to be or do you need to course-correct?

NOTE: I'm not suggesting you ignore the past, just don't get trapped in a fanciful gaze. Focus on today forward while recognizing prior missteps so you can minimize them while moving ahead. For example, beating yourself up over not having contributed more each month is of no help, but it would be quite productive to use that observation as an incentive to increase your go-forward contributions.

You may be a Gen Z coming of age, or a millennial with oppressive student debt, or a boomer playing catch-up, but the process is the same for all of us: PCR: Plan, Course-Correct, Repeat. Think about what to do, go do it, then do as little as possible after that! And it's not overly time-consuming. A handful of hours *per year* is all we are talking about.

YOU CANNOT PREDICT THE FUTURE, BUT YOU CAN MAKE EDUCATED, REASONABLE ASSUMPTIONS

Quite assuredly some of your assumptions will prove to be wrong, and over time specific goals will change. Life happens and that's OK. Course-correct. By doing this modeling every year you effectively force yourself to course-correct for prior erroneous assumptions (your personal "one-degree" errors). This is because you start each year's model with the actual balance in your FI Portfolio, and no matter the reason for not meeting the prior year's projection (returns were less; you missed some monthly contributions; emotionally forced errors, etc.), you reset as of today. This means the today-forward projection will by default compensate for any cumulative prior missteps or changing goals. Or it may alternatively show that you are ahead of schedule. In this case, keep it up!

For example, let's say you started the year with some amount of savings and a 15-year plan to grow it to $1 million. The plan *projected* you'd be at $100,000 by the end of the current year, but your *actual* FI Portfolio balance turns out to be only $92,000 because the markets didn't cooperate. Well, now you start the revised model with $92,000 and only 14 years to go to your targeted FI date. Since your targeted goal is still $1 million, your plan will effectively need to make up the $8,000 shortfall over the remaining 14 years in your plan. Maybe you increase your monthly contributions, push out your FI date by a year or two, etc. This is course-correcting.

If you continuously use assumptions that are too aggressive, you will continuously have major course corrections. This cycle of self-correcting every year will eventually lead you to refine your projected assumptions and goals so that the next year's course correction isn't quite as drastic. After all, a well-designed plan not followed is simply a lie wrapped in an excuse.

Doing this exercise every year is also a good means to hold yourself (and any advisor) accountable. When you accurately measure results and accept responsibility, things almost always improve.

"When you reach for the stars you might not quite get one. But you won't come up with a handful of mud either."

—LEO BURNETT

With so many variables and long-time horizons, at best these models are educated guesses. No model (or person) can predict the future with anything even approaching complete accuracy. They just can't be that precise. But they can be very good directional indicators. And the better you refine the assumptions and goals (monthly contributions, desired monthly withdrawals, expected returns, etc.), the more useful the output will be.

> **NOTE:** There are more dynamic planning tools out there known as Monte Carlo simulators. They effectively take the simplified static model above and make it dynamic by running thousands (sometimes tens of thousands) of variations with slight changes to the multitude of variables each time. The output is the probability that the plan works measured by the percentage of time the scenarios don't run out of monthly withdrawals. For example, if the simulator runs 5,000 scenarios and in 500 of them you run out of money, the simulator would conclude that your plan has a 90% likelihood of succeeding. Most professional advisors use Monte Carlo simulators and some offer a free version for consumers. As an example, check out Vanguard's Retirement Nest Egg Calculator.[4]

Run the model several times with slight changes to inputs to get a better sense of the variability of potential outcomes. It will help inform your spending bucket allocations and FI Portfolio decisions with a holistic perspective.

If you have no idea currently what your monthly withdrawal needs will be years from now, that's okay. Go back to Chapter One and add up spending Buckets B, C, and D. Your current spending is a good starting point for estimating your future spending/withdrawal needs. Then adjust as circumstances warrant. (For example, if your plan includes paying off your mortgage before your FI date, you can reduce your estimate of retirement monthly spending needs by subtracting the mortgage payment.)

I would target a spending goal higher than you currently think you will need. Most people I know over the age of 50 spend more than they envisioned when they projected out FI spending needs back in their 20s, 30s, and 40s. As you grow, life can get more complex and quite often more expensive.

"What is not started today is never finished tomorrow."
—JOHANN WOLFGANG VON GOETHE

Don't let the fact that you don't have a good estimate of future spending needs deter you. This modeling exercise will still be very informative. By looking at your Life's Complete Financial Arc, you can project out how much money per month you will have available to withdraw even though you don't know today if it will be sufficient (or excessive).

You should periodically compare that available withdrawal number to your evolving estimate of FI spending needs. Your task over time is to eventually get the two amounts (**available** withdrawals and **needed** withdrawals) to sync up. If they don't sync up, course-correct.

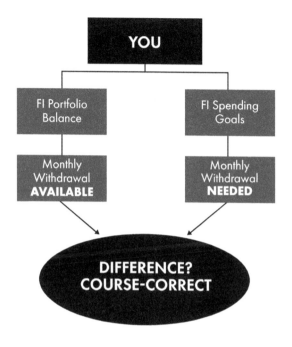

"*When the facts change, I change my mind. What do you do, sir?*"

—JOHN MAYNARD KEYNES

Goals (as well as your capacity for risk) will undoubtedly change over the years but the idea is to start somewhere and get moving. Create your plan and take action. Future course corrections will help adjust for those changing goals and the inevitable curveballs that life will throw at you.

For a good primer on retirement models (and a curated list of calculators) check out the book *Can I Retire Yet?* by Darrow

Kirkpatrick and/or visit his blog at CanIRetireYet.com. Kirkpatrick does an excellent job of explaining the strengths and shortcomings of calculators in general, as well as for each of the individual calculators he reviews.

Always remember, it's the planning process, not the plan, that will keep you sailing toward your goals. Whether you are at the beginning, middle, or end of your working career, this planning and modeling exercise will be quite illuminating.

One last question to ask yourself: you use over 2,000 hours every year working to make money, but how much time do you put into managing that money? Get out the oars and start rowing.

PCR: Plan, Course-Correct, Repeat.

SUGGESTIONS FOR ADDITIONAL READING

Darrow Kirkpatrick, *Can I Retire Yet?* (StructureByDesign, 2016).

Ramit Sethi, *I Will Teach You to Be Rich* (Workman Publishing Co., 2019).

3

BETTER THAN COMPOUND INTEREST

"Understanding both the power of compound interest and the difficulty of getting it is the heart and soul of understanding a lot of things."

—CHARLIE MUNGER

AS WE DEFINE (AND REFINE) OUR GOALS AND DESIGN A PLAN TO achieve those goals, we will continually invest our hard-earned money into that plan. A major tenet of such a plan is that we will invest in it for decades, and time will be a significant contributor to our success. But why is *time* so important?

24 HOURS A DAY

In 1976 the *Wall Street Journal* published an opinion column that ascribed an astounding revelation to one of the greatest minds in history. Albert Einstein was asked what he surmised to be man's greatest invention. He didn't respond with electricity or the wheel, but rather "compound interest."[5]

Variations on this theme include: Compound interest is the eighth wonder of the world. Compound interest is more complicated than relativity theory. Compound interest is the greatest mathematical discovery of all time. What could be better?

Regardless of whether Einstein said it, we should begin with understanding what compound interest is and why it is so amazing. Compound interest is the addition of interest to the principal sum of a deposit (or loan). Then, rather than being distributed, it is left in the account so that interest in the next period is earned on the principal plus previously accumulated interest. Simply put, you earn interest on your interest. Compound interest works 24 hours a day, 7 days a week, 52 weeks a year.

> **NOTE:** I should point out that compound interest works in both directions. When you borrow money, the interest you owe to the lender continues to accumulate 24 hours a day, 7 days a week, 52 weeks a year. Debt, per se, is neither bad nor good, but rather a powerful tool that comes at a cost you need to respect. So, remember this: Those who understand interest, earn it. Those who don't, pay it.[6]

Now let's expand this concept of compound interest by applying it to a hypothetical investment portfolio and examining a few alternative realities. Jasmine, a 27-year-old saver, places $20,000 in her fireproof safe locked away in the back of her closet and over the next 30 years never adds or removes one dollar from the safe. Thirty years later at age 57, Jasmine opens the safe, and waiting for her is her portfolio with a balance of exactly $20,000.

Alternatively, 27-year-old Jethro invests his $20,000 into an S&P 500 Index stock fund and manages to earn an annual return consistent with the stock market's long-term historical average, call it 10%. He also leaves the investment untouched for 30 years. That's 30 years of accumulating returns and watching the portfolio compound. At age 57, Jethro's initial $20,000 investment would have grown to almost $400,000, or 20 times more than what Jasmine has in the safe. That is the power of compounding that Einstein was referring to!

Future Portfolio Growth Example 1

	Year 0	Year 10	Year 20	Year 30
Jasmine	$20,000	$20,000	$20,000	$20,000
Jethro	$20,000	$54,592	$146,561	$396,748

Well then, what could be better than compound interest? It's what I like to refer to as compounding portfolio growth: leveraging the power of compound interest by combining it with regularly contributing new money to the portfolio.

Let's look at a third alternative reality for another young investor, Justine. She, like Jethro, starts with $20,000 invested in the S&P 500 fund. Each month, however, she takes the additional step of contributing $500 of new money to her S&P 500 fund. (This $500 per month could be achieved, for example, by funding her Roth IRA.) Thirty years later, assuming the same 10% average annual return, Justine would have more than $1.5 million in her portfolio. Justine turned $200,000 of contributions (the initial $20,000 plus $180,000 [$500 × 360 months]) into a $1.5 million portfolio or $1.1 million *more* than Jethro.

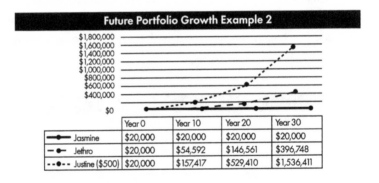

	Year 0	Year 10	Year 20	Year 30
Jasmine	$20,000	$20,000	$20,000	$20,000
Jethro	$20,000	$54,592	$146,561	$396,748
Justine ($500)	$20,000	$157,417	$529,410	$1,536,411

The combination of compound interest *and* new money contributions. That is the power of compounding portfolio growth. And THAT is better than compound interest by itself.

I've heard people say that it feels like they need to sacrifice too much today to come up with the incremental cash to invest each month. (A friend of mine often quips that all his cash is tied up in spare change!) I suggest they look at the challenge from a different angle. Don't think of it as sacrificing and saving. Think of it as spending today to buy your financial independence. Just ask yourself one question: "What am I willing to pay for it?" compounding portfolio growth—small incremental steps add up over time.

What if Justine could add $50 more each month to her portfolio? But $50 can't make that big a difference, right? Well, the numbers don't lie, and context matters. In the context of any given month, $50 is not likely to make a meaningful difference in Justine's lifestyle (after all, she's a dedicated, hardworking, well-compensated individual just like you).

In the context of her future portfolio 30 years hence, however, that $50 per month could increase her projected portfolio from $1.5 million to over $1.6 million. Think of it as simply this (using round numbers): EACH $50 per month (for 30 years) adds $100,000 to her future portfolio. If she recently received a pay raise and can increase her monthly investment by $250 ($750 in total), well, that could add another $500,000+ to her future portfolio bringing her total to $2.1 million.

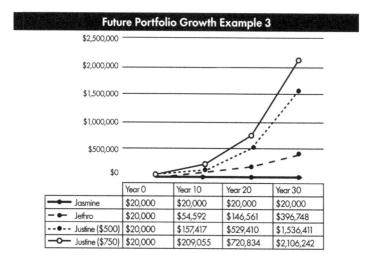

Future Portfolio Growth Example 3

	Year 0	Year 10	Year 20	Year 30
Jasmine	$20,000	$20,000	$20,000	$20,000
Jethro	$20,000	$54,592	$146,561	$396,748
Justine ($500)	$20,000	$157,417	$529,410	$1,536,411
Justine ($750)	$20,000	$209,055	$720,834	$2,106,242

Thinking about monthly contributions in terms of future portfolio value can bring to life for you the power of compounding portfolio growth. Start digging in your pocket for those extra $50s now. compounding portfolio growth—feed the beast.

Monthly contributions are the single most important tool in your investment toolbox, and when combined with an extended time frame, they are the secret sauce to compounding portfolio growth. In fact, during the first 10–15 years of your investing journey, your monthly contribution rate will have more of an impact on your wealth accumulation than will your investment rate of return. In the second half of your wealth accumulation journey, once you have a significant balance in your FI Portfolio, the rate of return will take on increasing importance.

> **NOTE:** Go back and highlight the previous paragraph. This is a critical fundamental concept worth repeating: during the first decade or so of your plan, maximizing your monthly contribution (and sticking to it) is more important than your rate of return!

Don't believe me? Let's assume you start your journey with zero dollars and create a portfolio that grows 5% per year. If you save 20% of your annual salary, in four and a half years your portfolio's value will exceed your annual income. Alternatively, if you got more aggressive, taking on more risk, and manage to grow 10% annually (double the rate of return in the first instance), you would get to the same portfolio value in four years and one month.

Said differently, the overwhelming majority of the portfolio growth in the early years is attributable to consistent monthly contributions, while increasing the growth rate (even doubling it in our example) shaved off less than 10% of the journey: 49 months down from 54 months. (It doesn't matter the dollar amount of annual income in this example; the math works the same regardless of the salary you start with.)

Back in 2000, a study on wealth accumulation noted that many Americans say they earn just enough to get by and struggle to get caught up on bills, implying they don't earn enough to also save money (not unlike today).

> Yet in other developed countries, the savings rate **at all income levels** is much higher than in the United States. Even in Canada—in many respects similar to the United States—the personal saving rate is almost twice as high as in the United States. Such international comparisons alone suggest that saving depends on much more than lifetime earnings.[7] (Emphasis added.)

While savings rates among countries have been shifting since this study was published, the key takeaway has not changed. Your savings rate is heavily dependent on your personal choices *and* is the single most important factor impacting your lifetime wealth accumulation.

Long periods of time require patience and the knowledge that the process is working, even when early on progress might appear to be coming painfully slow.

Look at the following chart, which uses hindsight to summarize Justine's wealth accumulation journey. Starting with her ending balance, we work backward to focus on how that balance accumulated over time. The chart references the total balance in her FI Portfolio at specific ages as a percentage of her final balance of $2.1 million (100% of her FI Portfolio at age 57).

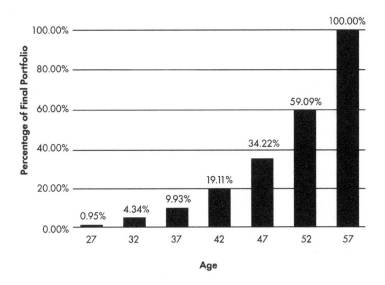

Justine's Wealth Accumulation by Age

So, for example, Justine started her FI journey at age 27 with $20,000, or less than 1% (0.95% to be exact) of her final balance. By age 42 she had accumulated 19% ($402,522/$2,106,242) of her final balance.

Said another way, 15 years (halfway) through her 30-year wealth accumulation journey, Justine had amassed less than 20% of her ultimate FI Portfolio balance. This means that 80% of her portfolio accumulation came in the second half of her journey. Looking closer, we see that over 40% of her total growth came in just the last five years (from age 52 to age 57)!

Even though Justine's example is a hypothetical journey, the accelerating trajectory is quite real. The early years of continuous contributions to the FI Portfolio quietly do their job in the background until they begin to show meaningful results in the second half of her journey. It's just how the math of exponential growth works.

The Psychology of Money, a book by Morgan Housel, provides a fascinating real-world example of the power of compounding. Warren Buffett started investing at the very young age of 10 years old, and by age 90, his net worth grew to $84.5 billion, $84.2 billion of which accumulated *after* his 50th birthday. Ninety-six percent of his wealth accumulated from his mid-60s on. That's compounding growth!

To help give the Buffett growth story some perspective, Housel considers a thought experiment. What if Buffett didn't start investing so early and jumped into the stock market at age 30 with $25,000 (not dissimilar to a lot of young adults these days)? And further, assume that from there Buffett was still able to achieve his phenomenal average return (roughly 22% annually) for 30 years, then quit investing to retire comfortably at age 60. According to Housel's calculations, Buffett's net worth would be approximately $11.9 *million*, or 99.9% less than his actual net worth.

As Housel points out, "Good investing isn't necessarily about earning the highest returns" because it's tough to consistently achieve those high returns. More importantly, you want to strive for reasonable returns that you can achieve more consistently over the long term.[8] And as the Justine example shows us, if you supercharge that good investing by contributing new money every month, well, that's when compounding portfolio growth can really skyrocket!

If I were to offer you a choice between receiving (1) $100,000 each day for 30 straight days, or (2) a penny that doubles every day for 30 days (day 1 = 1 penny, day 2 = 2 pennies, day 3 = 4 pennies, and so on), which would you take?

While it is simple linear math that lets you quickly value option 1 at $3 million (30 x $100,000), the compounding math of option 2 is not so easily calculated in your head with any precision. Let me offer some assistance. After 10 days you would have $5.12 worth of pennies. I hope you chose wisely.

From a mathematical perspective, the results for Justine, Buffett, and our penny example highlight the powerful implications of exponential growth (compound interest) versus linear growth (simple interest). They also highlight just how difficult it can be for us to wrap our heads around compounding. It's just not that intuitive. If you chose the penny that doubles, you would have $5.12 after 10 days, but you would finish day number 30 with almost $5.4 million! (Skeptical? Go ahead, start doubling the $5.12 20 more times.)

The Rule of 72 is a relatively effective cognitive shortcut that allows you to estimate one aspect of exponential growth: how long it will take to double your money at a specific rate of return. If you estimate a rate, you can calculate the years to double, and if you know the time period (number of years), you can calculate the rate needed to double your money.

For example, if your investment return is 8%, divide 72 by 8 and you get 9 years to double your money. Conversely, if you want to double your money in 10 years, divide 72 by 10 and you would need an annual investment return of approximately 7.2%.

But that's enough math talk. From a practical perspective, what does it means for us? Do not let the slow, seemingly motionless early years of compounding deter you. Stick to your plan, remain patient, and keep the faith that over the long term, compounding portfolio growth does work.

> **NOTE:** Don't bother looking beyond the Rule of 72 for mental shortcuts to calculate compounding growth scenarios; there are plenty of apps that can do the math for you. You will be much better served to focus your efforts on creating the mindfulness to accept as a mathematical given the power of compounding portfolio growth, and developing emotional fortitude to stick with it for the long term.

Warren Buffett is credited with the quote, "Life is like a snowball. The important thing is finding wet snow and a really long hill." Extending Buffett's concept, get behind the snowball (your portfolio) and give it a push. Get it rolling (invest early) and keep it rolling (by contributing each month) for a very long time.

SUGGESTIONS FOR ADDITIONAL READING

Morgan M. Housel, *The Psychology of Money* (Harriman House, 2020).

Todd Tresidder, *How Much Money Do I Need to Retire?* (Financial-Mentor, 2020).

4

MARKET RETURNS AND VOLATILITY

"Stability is not immobility."

—KLEMENS VON METTERNICH

IN ADDITION TO THE LACK OF INTUITIVENESS AROUND COMPOUND-ing portfolio growth, the volatility in market returns and your emotional responses can be a challenge to manage.

Let's go a little deeper on market returns and putting them in context. In March of 2009, the Great Recession was coming to an end with the S&P 500 Index bottoming out at 676. In late 2021, the Index is around 4,700, a rise of 595% over the 12+ years since the bottom. That's roughly a 16% compounded annual return. For a lot of you, those 12 years have been the majority of your investing experience. For more seasoned investors, it's getting easier and easier to forget the bears that came before this decade of fun. I know of no financial pundit, however, who would suggest these returns will continue unabated indefinitely. Diminishing returns and loss years in the stock market are inevitable. What should you do?

VOLATILITY IS INEVITABLE—WHETHER IT HURTS OR NOT IS UP TO YOU

When (not if) the next bear market arrives, your worst enemy will likely be you, or more specifically, your reaction. The best advice I can give you is to hurry up and do nothing. Don't panic. Don't overreact. Stick to your plan.

Trying to time the market (i.e., getting out before a drop and buying back in before a run-up) is a fool's errand, not to mention time-consuming and stressful. No one can predict the future. Jack Bogle, the founder of the Vanguard Group, wrote of market timing: "I don't know anyone who can do it successfully...Heck, I don't even know anyone who knows anyone who has timed the market with consistent, successful, replicable results."[9]

There have been numerous studies over the years laying out why market timers fail to consistently beat the market (especially over several-year periods). Nobel Laureate William Sharpe found that a market timer would have to be accurate 74% of the time to beat a passive portfolio at a comparable level of risk.[10] That is a high hurdle.

To illustrate that an investor's intuition and actions often prove to be counterproductive, famed economist Gene Fama once analogized money to a bar of soap: "The more you handle it, the less you'll have." The more frequently you check your portfolio, the more short-sighted and anxious to "do something" you are likely to become, especially during periods of extreme market volatility.

For an individual to profitably time the market, they must make not one but three correct decisions: (1) when to sell, (2) when to buy, and (3) what to do with the idle cash for the time in between (1) and (2).

ASSET ALLOCATION

Now that we understand why market timing is not for us, what are reasonable market return expectations for staying invested over the long term?

Using history as a guide (but not a guarantee for the future), projected average market returns are based on your personal asset allocation strategy. "Asset allocation" is simply a term used to describe what percentage of dollars in your FI Portfolio is invested in each category (asset class), such as stocks, bonds, real estate, etc.

Looking at two main asset classes, stocks and bonds, the following chart shows the range of returns and the variability in average returns (noted on top of each bar) across various stock/bond allocations.

Which asset classes should you invest in and what rate of return should you use to plug into the models we discussed in Chapter Two? As you can see, as the allocation to stocks increases so too does the average return. So, your gut reaction might be to pick the

Range of Returns for Different Asset Allocation Mixes (1926–2020) Bond% / Stock%

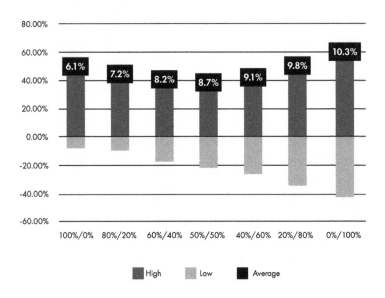

one with the highest average return (all stocks at 10.3%) and just go for it. Unfortunately, your choice isn't that simple. While stocks have delivered the greatest long-term results, they have also delivered the most dramatic swings both up and down. The 100% stock portfolio has ranged from its best year at 54.2% to its worst year down 43.1%!

If a 30–50% drop in the stock market would give you sleepless nights or drive you to sell as the market is crashing, then

100% in stocks is not a good idea. You need to balance expected returns with your personal level of stress inflicted when actual returns drift from expectations. You need to truly know yourself.

As we will continue to explore, invest in a mix of asset classes that gives you a strong probability of meeting your personal goals *and* that you can stick with when the inevitable stock market drops occur. And remember, nothing is forever. You can adjust your allocation as you progress on your FI journey.

> **NOTE:** See the Appendix for a list of stock and bond funds you might consider as a starting place for building your FI Portfolio and making asset allocation choices. I would suggest reviewing your asset allocation strategy no more than once per year. Don't worry about small ups and downs. Don't let asset allocation become the bar of soap Gene Fama referred to. Less is clearly more in this regard.

ONWARD AND UPWARD

Let's take a broader look at the market for context. In the following chart we see the past 120 years.

S&P Composite Index
Log Scale, Annual

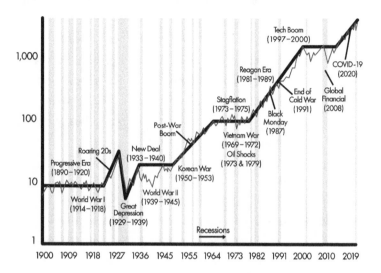

Source: JP Morgan's Guide to the Markets Q2 2021[11]

The vertical gray lines represent recessionary periods, the most recent being the dot-com bust in 2001, the meltdown during the 2008 financial crisis, and the COVID-19 pandemic. But notice this: through all the economic setbacks, wars, and dozens of recessions, the market's trend line over the 120 years is upward. If you believe, as I do, that America's economy and the global markets will continue upward *over the long term,* then in the short term, stay the course.

At a high level, calendar year stock market returns have been positive approximately 75% of the time over the last 100 years. That's an average of three out of every four years. More recently, from 1980 through 2020, the stock market (S&P 500) has delivered positive price returns 76% of the time (31 out of those 41 years).

But across those 41 years, the market had an intrayear average *decline* of 14.3%.[12] This means that even in the 31 calendar years with positive returns, significant declines occurred at some point during the year. Case in point, 2020 finished the year with a positive 16% return, but during the year suffered through a 34% decline.

The odds are on your side for being invested over the long term with a healthy dose of stocks, and recognizing that volatility in the short term makes timing the market a loser's game. Stick to your long-term plan. Stay the course.

> *"It's always darkest just before the day dawneth."*
>
> **—THOMAS FULLER**

It's important to not discount human ingenuity and resiliency. As history demonstrates, we have been through one crisis after another, but the entrepreneurial spirit never ceases to burn bright. Down cycles spur creative thinking and innovation. Necessity is often the mother of invention. New ideas and new companies spring forth even in the most dire of times.

GE was launched in 1892 by Thomas Edison right at the start of the Panic of 1893, which brought an end to America's "Gilded Age."

GM was launched in early 1908 by founder William Durant amid the Panic of 1907, which saw the New York Stock Exchange fall almost 50%.

In 1928, brothers Walt and Roy Disney introduced the world to Mickey Mouse. In 1929, just as the Great Depression started, the brothers incorporated Walt Disney Productions.

Federal Express Corporation was launched by Fred Smith in 1971 at the end of the 1969–1970 recession. Though the recession was relatively mild, Smith faced many challenges in trying to get the business community to accept as reliable a door-to-door cargo delivery service that eventually became known around the world as simply FedEx.

An oil crisis and stock market crash in 1973 led to a 16-month-long bear market. By December of 1974, the Dow Jones Industrial Average had declined 45%. In April 1975, Bill Gates and Paul Allen, undeterred by the recent economic collapse, launched their computer software company, Microsoft.

And out of the Great Recession of 2008–2009, we saw the launch of creative businesses like Uber, Venmo, Square, and Instagram.

"Courage is being scared to death, but saddling up anyway."

—JOHN WAYNE

If you have the intestinal fortitude to keep investing right through a bear market, your portfolio will reap the benefit. In fact, you will make most of your long-term portfolio gains during bear markets. You just won't recognize that fact until after the bear market passes. Patience and discipline are key virtues when it comes to long-term investing. And like the entrepreneurs that came before us, you also need to learn to look fear in the eye and not flinch.

Design and periodically review your investment plan; make regular contributions; and stick to the plan especially when extreme market volatility sets in. Let the power of compounding portfolio growth pull you through turbulent times. PCR: Plan, Course-Correct, Repeat. Your future self will undoubtedly thank you.

SUGGESTIONS FOR ADDITIONAL READING

Marin Katusa, *The Rise of America: Remaking the World Order* (Katusa Research Publishing, 2021).

5

SHOULD YOU HIRE
AN ADVISOR?

*"A banker is a fellow who lends you his umbrella when the
sun is shining, but wants it back the minute it begins to
rain."*

—MARK TWAIN

JOKES ASIDE, I USED TO BELIEVE, CATEGORICALLY, THAT PAYING
someone else to do what you can do yourself is wasted money. I
have also experienced enough to have learned "never say never."
Just because you can physically climb a two-story ladder and paint
the exterior of your house doesn't mean you should.

Some of us can build, invest in, and manage on our own an FI
plan across our Life's Complete Financial Arc. Others find the task
daunting, unsettling, and even scary. And a lot of us fall somewhere in between. Paying an advisor to help you get started with

some or all of the planning process and keep you on course is a whole lot better than never getting started at all.

THE PROCESS OF ACCUMULATING WEALTH IS SIMPLE, BUT NOT EASY

As we discussed in Chapter Three, accumulating wealth with compounding portfolio growth is quite a simple concept. It just takes time, discipline to stick with your monthly contributions, and patience to let it work. Most of the time it's quite boring. And therein lies the rub.

In a world where waiting two whole days for an Amazon package to arrive on the front doorstep is becoming downright annoying, sticking with a plan for decades, even a simple and boring plan, can be a monumental challenge to your endurance. If the multidecade timeline isn't tough enough, mix in some precipitous drops in the stock market like the March 2020 gut-wrenching 30% plummet, as well as daily the-sky-is-falling headlines. Now how do you feel? The combination—decades of time and wild market swings—can wreak havoc on your psyche.

For those of you who just can't manage the emotional and endless roller-coaster ride that is the stock market, what if an advisor could help you with a financial plan and keep you on course to (and through) financial independence—how much would you be willing to pay for their assistance?

Let's set out this threshold understanding. The person you hire is your business advisor, not a magician or dictator. What business, you ask? The business of accumulating and managing your wealth throughout your Life's Complete Financial Arc. Your advisor is effectively an employee of your business. You set the course with input from your advisor and you manage the plan with some tasks (of your choosing) delegated to your advisor. In other words, you run the business with or without the hired help of advisors.

> *"Economic forecasting exists to make astrology look respectable."*
>
> **—JOHN KENNETH GALBRAITH**

First, understand that advisors cannot forecast the markets, nor predict future stock or fund performance. They cannot guarantee investment results. If they tell you they can, find another advisor.

Now, let's separate the activities or roles an advisor can provide you into three broad areas: (1) investment selection, (2) financial planning, and (3) financial coaching. We'll discuss each of them in turn.

> *"All the time and effort that people devote to picking the right fund, the hot hand, the great manager, have in most cases led to no advantage."*
>
> **—PETER LYNCH**

In 2007, Warren Buffett offered to wager $500,000 that no investment professional could select a group of at least five hedge funds that would over 10 years beat the performance of an unmanaged low-cost Vanguard S&P 500 Index fund (with winnings to be donated to charity). Although there are thousands of professional investment managers, only one stepped up to accept the bet. ("Only one" says a lot in and of itself.) Ted Seides, co-founder of hedge fund Protégé Partners, accepted the wager and chose five fund-of-funds (which in turn invested in over 200 hedge funds). Seides's results would be averaged and compared to Buffett's S&P 500 fund. The bet ran from 2008 through 2017.

At the end of the 10 years, Seides's hedge funds averaged a gain (net of fees) of almost 3% per year. Buffett's S&P 500 Index fund averaged 8.5% per year. In fact, except for 2008, the group of hedge funds trailed the Index fund every single year. In dollars, the hedge funds grew the $500,000 to about $700,000, while Buffett's fund more than doubled it to almost $1.2 million.[13]

Why did I tell you this story? Odds are that a financial advisor who *only* focuses on picking investments for you will struggle to add measurable value over the long term compared to low-cost, broad-based index funds. The Buffett bet makes for a good story but was he just lucky? Let me provide some more data for you to chew on.

For the last 19 years, Dow Jones has published its SPIVA Scorecard (S&P Indices Versus Active), which compares the performance of actively managed equity mutual funds to their appropriate index benchmark. The report observes that the index versus active fund debate has been a "contentious subject for decades" and there are impassioned believers on both sides,[14] but the data reveals a compelling story.

The Scorecard found that over the 20-year period (2001–2020), 94% of large-cap managers, 88% of mid-cap managers, and 88% of small-cap managers lagged their respective benchmarks:

Report 1: Percentage of US Equity Funds Underperforming Their Benchmarks

Fund Category	Comparison Index	1-Year (%)	3-Year (%)	5-Year (%)	10-Year (%)	20-Year (%)
All Domestic Funds	S&P Composite 1500	57.09	67.01	72.80	83.22	86.01
All LargeCap Funds	S&P 500	60.33	69.71	75.27	82.32	94.00
All MidCap Funds	S&P MidCap 400	50.68	53.49	59.68	72.80	88.03
All SmallCap Funds	S&P SmallCap 600	45.52	57.04	65.12	76.31	88.06

Source: SPIVA Scorecard[15]

What about more recently—for example, calendar year 2018 when the S&P 500 Index lost 4.4%, or 2019 when the Index was up 30%? How did the funds actively managed by investment professionals fare? Over two-thirds of all domestic funds lost more in 2018 and delivered less in 2019.

> **NOTE:** Even if you are lucky enough to select today's market-beating fund, chances are it won't stay that way for long. Less than 2% of all equity funds remained in the top quartile over the five years 2016–2020, and not one multi-cap fund was able to do so.[16]

Over the long-term investment horizon, such as 10 or 20 years, more than 80% of active managers across all categories under-performed their respective benchmarks. Let me offer a corollary to that statement: investing in broad-based index funds can get your performance in the top 20%. Not bad for "only" matching the market's average results.

> **NOTE:** I bet you don't like to think of yourself or anything in your life as "average." In this context, we're not talking about the mathematical middle of the road, but rather achieving the combined performance of all the companies in the Index—placing your performance in the top 20% of all active fund managers. From this perspective, "average" is an excellent result!

A fascinating study by Arizona State University professor Hendrik Bessembinder found that across 25,300 publicly listed companies from 1926 to 2016 (a 90-year period), just five companies (Exxon, Apple, Microsoft, GE, and IBM) accounted for 10% of total share-holder wealth creation. And quite remarkably, the professor found that just 4% of all companies accounted for 100% of the net gain for the entire stock market from 1926 to 2016.[17] Said another way, the remaining 96% of companies collectively generated lifetime gains that merely matched gains on one-month Treasury bills.

Dig a little deeper into Bessembinder's findings, and you'll see that common stocks also tend to have rather short lives. The median time a stock is listed is just 7.5 years, and the single most frequently observed outcome for individual common stocks over their full lifetimes is a loss of 100%.

> **NOTE:** Jeff Bezos, founder of Amazon, homed in on the fact that no company lasts forever. In an all-hands meeting, Bezos told employees that the company is not too big to fail. "I predict one day Amazon will fail. Amazon will go bankrupt. If you look at large companies, their lifespans tend to be 30-plus years, not hundred-plus years."[18]

Others have similarly noted that excess returns observed for broad equity portfolios (for example, the S&P 500 Index) are attributable to relatively few stocks.[19] A minority of stocks in an index deliver the positive results that drive up the average, which means the majority of remaining stocks deliver less than the average result. (As I write this, just five companies account for 21% of the S&P 500 Index: Apple, Microsoft, Amazon, Facebook, and Alphabet.)

So, if you (or an active fund manager) attempt to cherry-pick a subset of S&P 500 stocks, recognize this: every stock you choose has an equal chance of being above the median, but since the drivers of the Index's positive return are skewed to a select few companies, each company has much less than a 50/50 chance of being above average.

These findings of skewed returns highlight the importance of port-folio diversification for most investors—holding a broad-based basket of investments. Unless, of course, you have a comparative advantage that can identify *in advance* the few individual stocks that will generate the highest long-term positive returns going forward. (Remember: over 80% of active fund managers do not demonstrate such an advantage.)

As the Buffett bet and the research demonstrate, the odds of consis-tently beating the market are stacked against you. This doesn't mean, however, that you can't endeavor to do better than average (i.e., "beat the market") with actively managed funds, individual stock selections, and your keen investment prowess. Just be sure to understand both the probability of success and the risk profile of the investments you and your advisor research and ultimately invest in.[20]

While you might shoot to outperform the market with a piece of your portfolio, I (along with the data) would suggest that "beating the market" should not be the bedrock on which you build your financial future.

To paraphrase the Disney song "Let It Go": Let the index vs. active storm rage on. The debate never bothered me anyway.

"It's important to have a plan, a big picture. You can deviate from it or change it completely, but it gives you something to work for."

—SHANNON MILLER

As we've discussed, financial planning, however, is much broader than just picking investments and measuring returns. It should help you achieve the ultimate financial goal we set out in Chapter One: financial independence, which will generate monthly cash flow you don't outlive. So, the role of an advisor can be broader as well.

In addition to assisting with investment choices, some advisors can help with plan design; cash flow planning including monthly contributions, then monthly withdrawals; periodic status check-ups against plan; course-correcting; tax efficiency; legacy planning; survivor assistance after you're gone, etc. These are but a few of the valuable financial planning actions an advisor can provide to your business.

But even if you hire one or more advisors, you can't abdicate complete responsibility. Assessing the plan, reviewing results and the outlook, understanding how the advisor is compensated (including the why and how much you are paying them), and at least a rudimentary understanding of the investments are all your continuing responsibility.

As the owner of the business, you can choose to outsource plan design, and even plan execution, but overall strategy approval, that's on you. Whether you develop the plan on your own or with the assistance of an advisor, you need to "own" the plan and its path to FI. This is your business, and no one will care about your business (and your money) as much as you do.

"Son, you've got a good engine, but your hands aren't on the steering wheel."

—BOBBY BOWDEN

"Financial coach." Think of all that might entail: consultant, mentor, motivator, teacher, organizer, therapist...

Over the years, several studies have tried to quantify the benefit of using an advisor vs. self-directing your portfolio. Estimates of the benefit are as high as 4%. One such analysis at the high end of the range, Vanguard: Quantifying Advisor's Alpha,[21] estimates the "Alpha" (excess return over a market benchmark) can be, *on average,* approximately four percentage points on top of what an individual could achieve on their own. Sounds impressive but let's peel back the layers a little bit. First, back out the average advisory fee (implied 1% in the study) to get to a net, 3%. Next, there is roughly 0.6% benefit attributable to simply helping you choose and rebalance low-cost funds. Today, fund expenses are now prominently disclosed and easy enough for anyone to see.

Most of the remaining Alpha is related to two areas: (1) helping you with your cash withdrawal strategy (up to 1.1%), and (2) keeping you from yourself! (1.5%). The Vanguard study goes on to explain that the value of a "simple" plan is in helping the investor more easily endure the volatility in the markets, keeping investors grounded when wild headlines and their own emotions tempt them to dump their investment plan. Simply put, the majority of Alpha resides not in investment selection, but rather in behavioral coaching.

Quantifying this Alpha associated with keeping you from making suboptimal financial decisions is not easily reduced to a number or percentage, especially when sometimes it's the actions you choose *not* to take that count more. But the benefit can be real nonetheless.

There is enormous value in financial planning and charting your course to financial independence. Even if your investment results trail the market, your business stays focused on the ultimate financial goal. You may lose the annual market-beating battle, but you (and your advisor) are focused on winning the FI war.

ADVISORY SERVICE FEES

Some advisors work for a flat fee or rate per hour agreed to up front with the investor. A common fee structure among personal financial advisors is a fee based on a percentage of the value of your portfolio that the advisor manages, commonly referred to as assets under management (AUM). A typical fee might be, say, 1% of AUM calculated and paid at regular intervals (e.g., quarterly or annually).

> **NOTE:** While a percentage of AUM generally aligns both your interests (i.e., you both gain as the portfolio grows), it's not a perfect alignment. Paying this type of fee promotes maintaining the pot and you adding to the pot, but not necessarily profitable results. For example, if you ask your advisor if you should invest more or pay down your mortgage, the answer should be based on what's best for you,

> but recognize that the former will increase their fee while the latter will not. Hence the old adage: you should not ask a barber if you need a haircut.

Your lawyer, accountant, landscaper, hairstylist, and doctor are all paid for their services but not necessarily the outcome. You then evaluate (consciously or subconsciously) that service and decide whether to engage the same service provider in the future. You should evaluate the service you receive from, and fees you pay to, your financial advisor in much the same manner.

> **NOTE:** Don't be short-sighted, however, in your assessment. For example, making short-term monthly or quarterly investment comparisons for what is a robust long-term plan might prove to be counterproductive. But they are data points nonetheless and could be used in conjunction with other inputs as you have a dialogue with your advisor. The key is periodic and ongoing touch points with your advisor to ensure you are both on the same page and accountable to each other—the basis for a trusting relationship.

Here is a suggestion for creating your personalized benchmark (*one* of the criteria you could use to evaluate the investment performance component of your portfolio). Bifurcate your monthly FI Portfolio contribution into two parts: 90% of the contribution to be actively managed by your advisor and the remaining 10%

self-directed by you alone and invested in a low-cost, broad-based index fund(s) (for example, Vanguard's Total Stock Market Index Fund [VTI], and/or if you want to focus on the large-cap segment of the total market, the Vanguard S&P 500 ETF [VOO]).

The reason I suggest using your own 10% account is to reflect what you actually do on your own rather than using a hypothetical comparison to "market returns." Unlike published market rates of return, your 10% account return will factor in your monthly contributions, any trading activity or withdrawals, one-time contributions, what you do with dividends, etc. Rather than guessing what you can do on your own, you will know for sure. And be sure to do this comparison (10% account vs. advisor-managed account) net of fees so that you have an apples-to-apples comparison.

PERFORMANCE COMES AND GOES, BUT EXPENSES ARE THE GIFT THAT KEEP ON GIVING (TO THE FUND MANAGER)

In researching some data for this chapter, I conducted an informal (and clearly unscientific) survey of a few individual investors. For the subset of investors using an advisor, I asked them how their advisor is compensated. Most of the investors were quick to point out that their advisor does not earn commissions, and is charging "only 1%." When I then asked if they knew the actual dollar amount (as opposed to the percentage) paid last year, everyone paused and did some mental gymnastics to estimate the dollars (even though it was a simple yes/no question). Not one investor knew the actual dollars paid since the fee is unceremoniously subtracted from their portfolio balance.

Let's peer into the future. You have worked hard your entire
career and have used compounding portfolio growth in conjunc-
tion with your advisor to grow your portfolio from $200,000 to
reach financial independence with an impressive $3 million port-
folio. The advisory fee you were paying in the beginning, $2,000
per year, has also been growing. The "only 1%" advisory fee you
are now paying is $2,500 *per month*. (This fee is likely one of your
largest monthly expenses, but is it a line item in your spending
budget?)

I'm willing to bet that if you had to Venmo $2,500 to your financial
advisor each month, you'd consciously make sure you understood
why. Just because you don't write a check shouldn't eliminate your
desire to understand, appreciate, and periodically evaluate the
"why."

> **NOTE:** Bestselling financial author Charles D. Ellis proposes
> that fees should more appropriately be based on a percent-
> age of returns instead of assets. More accurately, as a
> percentage of incremental returns–above what you can do
> on your own. You are putting up 100% of the capital and
> taking all the risk, so why are fees paid regardless of the
> advisor's actual performance?[22] A laudable proposal, but
> I'm not aware of any money managers revising their fee
> structure to follow Mr. Ellis's suggestion.

If you choose to hire an advisor, ask yourself this question: are the
returns (financial and behavioral) above what you can do on your
own and more than enough to cover the advisory fee? To answer

the question, you need to benchmark your advisor *and* be honest with yourself with respect to your own behavioral shortcomings.

For a lot of people, investment selection alone might not justify the whole fee, but combined with holistic planning and behavioral coaching, the fee might very well be worth it.

GOOD (AND NOT SO GOOD) ADVISORS MANAGE PEOPLE'S MONEY; GREAT ADVISORS MANAGE PEOPLE AS WELL AS THEIR MONEY

When searching for an advisor, titles alone might not be of much help. There is unfortunately a plethora of financial monikers to choose from. Some are helpful and some may be of limited value. There is no standard title for the holistic planner (all three areas we discussed above). Some call themselves investment advisors, life planners and financial coaches, financial life planners, wealth management advisors, investment consultants, personal advisors, or just financial advisors. They may be credentialed (or not) as a certified financial planner, chartered financial analyst, or personal financial specialist, or have other credentials.

If you are using an advisor or considering hiring an advisor, I'd suggest talking with friends and reading up on the topic. To get you started, the University of Illinois has a good summary entitled *Consumer Guide to Choosing a Financial Professional.*[23]

Financial author and certified financial planner Carl Richards lays out three simple reasons that artfully sum up why he has an advisor (and they are also a good sanity check for the rest of us):

1. Help me clarify my goals.

2. Remind me of my goals.

3. Stand between me and stupid.[24]

Before I wrap up this chapter, do me a favor. Pause here and answer the following question: this chapter is advocating for (1) self-reliance, or (2) working with an advisor?

Although my proclivities often come through in my writing, my overarching goal with this book is to help you with *how* to think about personal finance matters, not *what* to think. I hope you, therefore, looked past the binary choice you were presented and came up with (3) making a better-informed decision that meets your personal needs.

It is the same choice as going to the gym on your own or with the assistance of a personal trainer. Any way you slice it, you are the one breaking a sweat.

SUGGESTIONS FOR ADDITIONAL READING

Carl Richards, *The Behavior Gap: Simple Ways to Stop Doing Dumb Things with Money* (Penguin Publishing Group, 2012).

John C. Bogle, *The Little Book of Common Sense Investing: The Only Way to Guarantee Your Fair Share of Stock Market Returns* (John Wiley & Sons, 2017).

6

BEATING THE MARKET

"Where all think alike, no one thinks very much."

—WALTER LIPPMANN

As we have discussed, our primary FI goal is to meet our annual spending requirements without the need to expend our labor to generate cash flow. Yet, many of us just love comparing investment results, recounting stories of big "wins," and bragging about beating the market.

Consistently outperforming the market is but a dream for most investors. In the previous chapter, we learned that a vast amount of data shows us that beating the market over the long term is an elusive endeavor for novices and professionals alike. But why is it that so few investors can do it, and so many more attempt it but come up short?

One explanation may reveal itself if we gain a better understanding of the opponent every individual is trying to best. Rest assured you are up against a worthy opponent—the average investor.

Beating the market is a significant challenge, but not an impossible one. A few professionals have done it across various periods and to varying degrees of success. Names that quickly come to mind include the likes of Buffett, Soros, Simons, Templeton, Gross, Klarman, Marks, Graham, Lynch, and Ackman. Each has managed to do it over varied periods of time and garnered notable media attention, which only adds to the allure of taking up the challenge.

So, how do you go about beating the market? For starters, if the market and you think the same way about an investment, then it's likely that the asset price already reflects the future everyone collectively envisions. If the market, however, doesn't think the same *and* your assumptions are correct, then the investment could be mispriced (under-/overvalued), providing you with an investable opportunity. Being an accurate contrarian is where you will make more money than the average investor, not following the herd.

Thinking differently sounds simple enough, but is it? Howard Marks is the co-founder of Oaktree Capital Management, an investment firm with over $75 billion under management. In his thought-provoking book *The Most Important Thing Illuminated*, he explores this concept of thinking differently.

Not only does your investment thesis need to be right, Marks observes, it must be "more right than others."[25] He describes this ability to think differently and better as "second-level thinking." It's about evaluating your investment thesis *relative* to the market's view of the same opportunity.

Buying a stock because you think the price will go up (its fundamentals are strong, great products, future looks bright, etc.) is first-level thinking. Buying it because you've developed an investment thesis that others don't see is second-level thinking. It almost doesn't matter what you think in isolation; it matters more what you think in relation to what others believe.

A first-level thinker might say that they expect the company to beat its guidance for the next quarter's revenue, driving the stock price up, so it's time to buy. A second-level thinker would push to understand "why" the spike in revenue—e.g., a one-time large sale, which means longer-term revenue will likely come back down and it's time to reevaluate and maybe sell.

SUCCESS COMES FROM STANDING APART, NOT HOLDING HANDS WITH THE CROWD

Getting to the second level requires deeper analysis, exploration of complex and interrelated assumptions, and uncovering unique insights. It's about pushing yourself to keep asking, "Why?," "What's next?," "What could go wrong?" Second-level thinking is time-consuming and hard work, much harder than first-level thinking.

If you get your financial news from the 24-hour news cycle (Twitter feeds, CNBC, etc.) and you don't go any deeper to ask probing questions and form contrarian views, then you are quite likely forming first-level thinking opinions with information available to all investors. Thinking the same as the market consensus is generally not the path to outperforming that same market.

TIME TO GO SHOPPING

If you have convinced yourself that you have the time, energy, and skillset to achieve second-level thinking and the conviction to act upon it, who is this average investor that you are looking to outsmart? Let's step back and put the market and the average investor into perspective.

What is the stock market? When you need groceries, you go to the supermarket. When you want to buy stocks or funds, you go to the stock market. It's merely a meeting place (mostly digital these days) for willing buyers and willing sellers to come together to trade (buy and sell) securities.

In general terms, there are two main "categories" or types of markets: the primary market and the secondary market. When a company sells stock shares and bonds to the public for the first time, it does so in the primary market. Often, the new issues take the form of an initial public offering (IPO). Also, existing public companies may raise more capital by issuing (selling) new shares in a follow-on offering. In the US both forms of stock sales by companies are heavily regulated by the Securities and Exchange Commission.

It is widely accepted that a foundational rationale for Wall Street and the financial markets is to efficiently provide capital to businesses, commonly referred to as capital formation: providing new money for companies to develop new products, expand into new businesses, explore new technologies, modernize existing plants and equipment, etc.

In the primary market, the important thing to understand is that investors are making the purchase directly from the company, and in doing so providing the company with new capital to fund its business operations.

The secondary market, on the other hand, is where securities are generally traded between investors without the companies' involvement. Think of the secondary market as the eBay for stocks. For example, if you purchase Apple stock, you are buying it from a selling investor who owns the shares. Apple is not directly involved with this trade. This secondary market for equities is more commonly referred to as the stock market. Examples of secondary markets include the New York Stock Exchange, the Nasdaq, Japan Exchange Group, and the London Stock Exchange, to name just a few.

Up until the mid-20th century, companies were selling shares to mostly retail investors (individual, nonprofessional investors) to raise cash to grow their businesses. Those retail investors were more than willing to hold onto those stock purchases and collect dividends, with capital appreciation being a potential by-product but not a primary goal.

In recent decades, however, long-term investing by mostly individuals has given way to short-term trading. At one point, Jack Bogle, Vanguard founder, calculated that IPOs and secondary offerings in the US averaged about $250 billion over the previous five years. Stock trading in the secondary market averaged $33 trillion. So, of the total market activity, trading accounts for 99.2% while capital formation is just 0.8%.[26] The stock markets have become a collection of investors and speculators incessantly trading stocks back and forth with each other.

WHO IS THE AVERAGE INVESTOR DOING ALL THIS TRADING?

In 1950, retail investors owned over 90% of the stock of US corporations, but the times have been changing. Across the globe, institutional investors now hold more than 40% of global market capitalization, and that percentage is a lot higher in some of the more developed markets. For example, in the United Kingdom, almost two-thirds (63%) of the equity capital of public companies is owned by institutional investors. In the US, institutions own 72%.[27]

Retail investors who were, up until the mid-20th century, the primary drivers of the stock market now take a back seat to institutional behemoths. Almost 85% of the world's largest public companies have a single shareholder who owns more than 10% of the company's capital. The three largest shareholders hold more than 50% of the capital in half of the listed companies worldwide.[28]

With the breadth and depth of institutional stock ownership, especially in markets like the UK and the US, it's not a stretch to understand that the overwhelming majority of stock *trading* is also done by institutions.

As recently as 2010, trades by retail investors represented only 10% of US equity trading volume. Even with the proliferation of online brokers offering easy access and zero-commission trades, retail investors currently account for only a slightly larger share of total US trading volume—approximately 20% as of late 2021. Said another way, 80% of stock trading is still done by institutions.

Mutual funds, exchange-traded funds (ETFs), hedge funds, endowments, pension funds, REITs, insurance companies, venture capital funds, and sovereign wealth funds are examples of the types of institutions trading in the stock market. And the aggregate number of these institutional investors has continually grown. In the early 1950s, for example, the total number of US mutual funds was approximately 100. Today, there are 10,000 US mutual funds, a subset of the 122,000 mutual funds worldwide managing over $54 trillion in assets. It wasn't until 1990 that the first ETF was listed in Canada. Thirty years later ETFs number more than 7,000 globally with over $6 trillion in assets.[29]

And all these institutions employ thousands upon thousands of investing professionals—professionals that include chartered financial analysts (CFAs), certified financial planners (CFPs), MBAs, researchers, economists, and portfolio managers. And they often supplement their internal ranks by hiring a bevy of external advisors including lawyers, accountants, investment bankers, and acquisition specialists.

When George Soros, John Templeton, Jack Bogle, and Warren Buffett hit their stride in the investment business in the 1950s, do you know how many CFAs and CFPs they were up against? Precisely zero. It wasn't until 1963 that a total of 263 individuals—the original CFAs—were first accredited. Not until a decade later, in 1973, did the first CFPs arrive on the scene. Today there are more than 186,000 CFA professionals worldwide,[30] and more than 192,000 CFPs, with over 88,000 of them in the US.[31]

"Never give in except to convictions of honor and good sense."
                                        —WINSTON CHURCHILL

The bottom line: the competition in the marketplace has grown exponentially bigger, faster, more nimble, and (arguably) more intelligent over the last 70 years. Today, sophisticated institutions with massive computer power are running AI algorithms that can parse big data 24 hours a day. They have access to top professionals, unhampered by geographical boundaries, spending their entire working day, every day, looking for an investible advantage.

The market's average investor is an amalgamation that includes you, along with all the other individual investors, *plus* the collective wisdom, insights, and actions of all these institutions and professionals. It's no wonder that consistently beating the market, beating the composite average investor, is such an enormous challenge.

In any activity that involves both skill and luck, such as investing, as skill increases the vagaries of luck play an increasing role in the outcome. Financial author Michael Mauboussin describes this challenge as the Paradox of Skill.[32] This may sound counterintuitive, but it is explained this way: even if your skill is increasing, the skill of your competitors is likely also increasing (e.g., the average investor is a lot more skilled than they were decades ago). As everyone's actions and performance become more consistent, luck becomes more and more important.

Think about a professional tournament poker player in a game with amateurs and later in a second game with other top-ranked professionals. Skill will help the professional win over the amateurs. In the second game, since the skill level of all participants will be much closer to parity (all the professionals will know how to play each hand based on the odds), the actual cards dealt to them in any given hand (luck) will be of increasing consequence.

So, if you still endeavor to beat the market, please check your ego at the door, and don't confuse information with actionable knowledge. Information that everyone knows about is nice but doesn't necessarily provide an investible advantage. Even if you believe you have developed your second-level thinking investment thesis, realize that the average investor is waiting to take the opposing view and trade with you.

And when you realize how difficult it is to be an above-average investor, you can focus some attention on avoiding the pitfalls that could land you below the average!

Even though you are a long-term investor, you occasionally find yourself with a need to trade stocks, but beating the market should not be your reason for doing so. You have a well-defined, long-term plan with personal goals along your Life's Complete Financial Arc. If a trade aligns with that plan, then and only then should you consider trading a stock.

SUGGESTIONS FOR ADDITIONAL READING

Howard Marks, *The Most Important Thing Illuminated: Uncommon Sense for the Thoughtful Investor* (Columbia University Press, 2013).

J. David Stein, *Money for the Rest of Us: 10 Questions to Master Successful Investing* (McGraw Hill Education, 2020).

Peter Lynch, *One Up on Wall Street* (Fireside, 1989).

John C. Bogle, *The Little Book of Common Sense Investing: The Only Way to Guarantee Your Fair Share of Returns* (John Wiley & Sons, 2017).

7

CONSTANT NOISE

"It's discouraging to think how many people are shocked by honesty and how few by deceit."

—NOËL COWARD

IN THE HARROWING EARLY DAYS OF THE COVID-19 PANDEMIC, a soothing letter was widely circulating on social media. It was purportedly written by F. Scott Fitzgerald in 1920 while quarantined in the south of France during the Spanish flu pandemic.

The letter, written with his characteristically lyrical phrasing, describes how he and his wife, Zelda, are hunkering down during the quarantine and stocking up on his favorite cocktails! It closes with Fitzgerald's inspiring hope for a better tomorrow.

The letter is humorous, poignant, hopeful, and an untruth. The words are true enough, they just weren't penned in 1920 or authored by F. Scott Fitzgerald. They were written in 2020 as a parody by humorist Nick Farriella.[33]

NOTE: Fitzgerald did write a letter to a friend in 1919 while hospitalized and perilously sick with influenza. He talked about isolation creating a "flow of sorrow" in him and developing a "horror of people."[34] No wonder the real letter didn't go viral—it's not nearly as uplifting as the parody.

As demonstrated above, people and facts can be skillfully parodied for entertainment purposes. But unfortunately, information can also be manipulated, intentionally or not, to support a point of view, or be misleading if presented out of context. On top of that, we as humans have an innate instinct to focus on the bad more than the good. During the early months of the COVID-19 pandemic, which did you notice more: the number of dead from the virus or the number of recovered?

PEOPLE JUST WANT TO BELIEVE

Sensationalized 24-hour news cycles, fueled by a crisis and our instinct for negative news, mean you need to do more than blindly accept every news screen banner and sound bite.

In one 24-hour period, I came across the following headlines: "Dow Jones Industrial Average futures pointing to a sharp triple digit drop." (With the Index around 24,000 at the time, 100 points are four-tenths of one percent.) "Dow drops more than 600 points as coronavirus shutdown slams economy." This was preceded 16 hours earlier by, "The Dow rose 559 points because good coronavirus news tops bad economic data." Are we less informed before reading these headlines or after?

Not blindly trusting everything does not equate to trusting nothing. People love a good story, but don't stop there. You need to step back, seek out perspective, and listen to and read multiple sources. Discuss with others and be open to opposing points of view. You simply need to be more discriminating and diligent in separating the truth from the noise, the meaningful from the irrelevant.

News, facts, and figures are food for the brain. And as my mother would constantly admonish me for rushing through dinner, "Chew your food, don't just swallow it whole!"

"This too shall pass."

—PERSIAN ADAGE

In March of 2020, the COVID-19 pandemic was racing around the globe and the US stock market was almost free-falling toward an eleven-year low. One late March morning, I received a text from a focused and dedicated investor that succinctly summarized how a lot of people were feeling about the stock market at the time: "I think I count as [a] disciplined [investor] but it still gives me agita looking at this disaster!"

Over the prior five years, through the day I received that text (which happened to be the market's 52-week low point), the S&P 500 had *risen* 440 points, which is an annual compounded return of roughly 4.5% (with dividends reinvested). Half of the market's long-term average rate of return, but not exactly disastrous, let alone agita-inducing.

I don't mean to diminish the precipitous month-long decline in the global markets induced by the awful spread of COVID-19, nor the social and political upheaval, but I do mean to say this: let's not lose our long-term perspective and give in to fear. Do not confuse the market's price volatility with the permanent loss of capital.

Let's look to the financial crisis of 2008–2009 for some additional perspective. By early 2008, Warren Buffett's personal ownership stake in Berkshire Hathaway stock had grown to an awe-inspiring $39 *billion*. Shortly thereafter, financial panic set in. By the time the "too big to fail" Wall Street crisis bottomed out in March of 2009, the market had driven Buffett's holdings down 41% to $23 billion.

How much did Buffett lose in the stock market? That's right, zero. He didn't lose $16 billion. He lost nothing—he didn't sell! He didn't need to withdraw his money; he believed his investments were high-quality businesses, and he didn't give in to fear and panic. In late 2021, the shares he didn't sell were priced at roughly $103 billion—over four times where they were in 2009.[35]

We live in a time when most "news" headlines and stories are more concerned with accumulating clicks than providing a balanced view of the facts. After all, media companies are in business to make money. And no matter the type of media we are talking about— news outlets, magazines, TV shows, social media, even movies— fear and bad news sell! Good news comes across as just ho-hum and hence is reported on far less frequently than bad news.

Fear not only drives advertising revenue to the media companies, it can also lead you to make rash decisions. A few months into the COVID-19 pandemic, I looked back at some news stories with headlines that can trigger the deepest of primal fears: "Market's 7-Day Rout Leaves US Reeling," "Worsening Crisis," "Mounting Fears Shake World Markets," "Financial Crisis Upends Campaign," "Dollar Falls Victim to Scramble for Safety," "Worst Week Ever for Stocks."

You must block out and see past all the noise. Believe in your plan, and the long-term viability of the global marketplace and the world's economic engine. Although at dire times it may very well get worse before it gets better, keep calm and carry on! Oh, by the way, the headlines quoted above were not from the COVID-19 pandemic of 2020, but from the darkest days of the 2008–2009 financial crisis 11 years earlier.

Stick to your plan.

SUGGESTIONS FOR ADDITIONAL READING

Hans Rosling, *Factfulness: Ten Reasons We're Wrong about the World—and Why Things Are Better than You Think* (Flatiron Books, 2018).

8

BE CAREFUL WHAT YOU PULL FROM THE RECYCLE BIN

"Science is organized knowledge. Wisdom is organized life."

—IMMANUEL KANT

ADVICE COMES AT US FROM ALL ANGLES AND WHEN IT COMES TO money, financial pundits and the financial press are hurling advice at us daily. How do we separate the wheat from the chaff?

When we seek out financial advice, we are looking for actionable wisdom that we can put to good use as we chart our course to financial independence. So, let's start with a common understanding of what "wisdom" is and how we might acquire it. Wisdom can be approximated with the following equation: ***Knowledge + Experience + Learning = Wisdom.***

KNOWLEDGE

Knowledge is the accumulation of basic facts and information, neatly stored and easily retrievable for later use. Gathering knowledge is a never-ending process, and reading is fundamental to that process. Be a sponge and absorb knowledge. Read, ponder, discuss, and read some more. Joseph Addison once observed, "Reading is to the mind what exercise is to the body."

EXPERIENCE

Over the 36 years I've been an investor, think about what we and our economy have been through: we have lived and worked through Black Monday in October of 1987, several wars and military actions, seven US Presidents (three Republican and four Democrat), the dot-com boom and the 2001 bust, the 2008 financial crisis, and the decade-long stock market euphoria suddenly shattered by a global pandemic, to name just a few. And if you are lucky enough to speak with someone with even more experience—for example, my 98-year-young mother—she would tell you all this stuff is just current events. Experiences add perspective and real-world sensibilities to knowledge.

LEARNING

Knowledge and experiences are of minimal value *unless* you use them to *learn*. Use them to gain a broader understanding, deeper insights, and new perspectives.

There are a lot of folks who have knowledge and years of experience but who fail to recognize the difference between quality decisions and simple luck. Or worse, they continually believe their decision-making skills are superior and their less-than-stellar track record is attributable to just bad luck. This apocryphal observation from Mark Twain comes to mind: "It ain't what you don't know that gets you into trouble. It's what you know for sure that just ain't so."

All your acquired knowledge and experiences shape views and inform decisions, and can be invaluable when making and course-correcting long-term investment plans. The ability to truly learn and extrapolate from experiences is what differentiates adults from children, intelligent investors from novices.

One hundred years ago, in his classic investment book *Reminiscences of a Stock Operator*, author Edwin Lefèvre offered timeless advice: "When you know what not to do in order not to lose money, you begin to learn what to do in order to win. Did you get that? You begin to learn!"

WISDOM

Wisdom is your ability to take your knowledge, experiences, and learning and shape them practically and productively to make good decisions throughout your lifetime. While knowledge is the accumulation of information, wisdom involves gaining perspective and insights, focusing on the meaningful and discarding the irrelevant, and using all the above to make well-reasoned judgments.

Two thousand five hundred years ago, Chinese philosopher Lao Tzu explained that the path to wisdom dictates that you "subtract" all irrelevant information and activities: "To attain knowledge, add things every day. To attain wisdom, subtract things every day." As we discussed in the previous chapter, "subtract" all the noise, and focus only on the meaningful.

Wisdom is your ever-expanding knowledge base wrapped in real-world experiences, filled with good and bad outcomes, idiosyncrasies, and "light-bulb" moments. Sometimes wisdom leads to big and bold insights. Other times, it can be so nuanced that if you're not paying attention, you'll look right past it.

Albert Einstein famously summed it up, "Wisdom is not a product of schooling but of the lifetime attempt to acquire it."

While you are making decisions based on wisdom, I encourage you to do it with a dose of humility. Humility to know and accept that despite all the wisdom you've accumulated, the good decision you make might result in a bad outcome.

> *"Doubt is an uncomfortable condition, but certainty is a ridiculous one."*
>
> **—VOLTAIRE**

Ian Wilson, former GE executive, offers a valuable insight: "No amount of sophistication is going to allay the fact that all of your knowledge is about the past and all your decisions are about the future."[36] A future that is unknown and unknowable. You can make informed decisions, well-reasoned assumptions, educated forecasts, but you still can't know the future. And when you pause to acknowledge that your investment thesis might prove to be wrong, it will nudge you away from aggressive assumptions and shoddy due diligence, and push you toward investments where the potential return is proportionate to the level of risk. Have a slice of humble pie; it will help you sleep better.

Let's be clear, a bad outcome does not necessarily mean you made a bad decision. And conversely, just because you achieve a good outcome doesn't mean you made a good decision.

In 2004, 32-year-old Ashley Revell sold all his possessions, gathered his life savings, left the UK, and flew to Las Vegas. He traveled to the Plaza Hotel and Casino to bet it all on a single spin of the roulette wheel. As a crowd gathered to watch, the ball was sent whirling around the wheel. He plopped down $135,000, his entire financial future, on red. Was this a good decision?

With a wave of his hand, the croupier announced no more bets. The ball slowed, then frantically bounced around, finally coming to rest on one number. The ball sat on red 7, doubling Revell's money to $270,000.[37] Tremendous outcome. Terrible decision.

> **NOTE:** I know the reaction of a few of you reading this is that Revell's roulette decision doesn't seem so terrible. So, my question to you is this: how many more times should Revell continue making this "good decision" of betting 100% of his net worth on a single spin of the wheel…and will you be doing the same?

If I play blackjack and I choose to hit on 20, any gambler will instantly know that I have statistically made a bad decision. If I happen to draw an ace and win the hand along with a stack of money, it was still a bad decision that happened to have a lucky outcome.

Like casino games, investing involves unknown facts influenced by random future events. Throughout your investing career, you will almost surely make some good decisions that turn out poorly— and vice versa. As my friend Rob likes to remind me, "Some days chicken, some days feathers."

The problem that people face is this tendency to evaluate the quality of a decision based solely on its outcome. This can lead investors to sometimes "learn" a flawed truth, the equivalent of "learning" that it's a good idea to hit on 20 in blackjack.

In the short term, a good outcome is wonderful. After all, it's tough to complain about winning! But it's dangerous if it leads an investor to conclude that their decision was sound and should be repeated. With an unknowable future, your goal is to use a well-thought-out decision process that puts you in a position with the best chance of a favorable outcome, *balanced* against the risk and cost of being wrong.

> **NOTE:** The quality of a decision is good or bad based on what was known at the time the decision was made, not on how it actually turned out. If you want the most objective evaluation of an investment thesis or any decision process, analyze it *before* you know the outcome.

Be wary of doing something just because it has worked well for you in the past. And be similarly cautious about discarding an idea just because it hasn't previously had a favorable outcome. Differentiate a good decision process from a lucky outcome. That's true wisdom.

> *"If you give a man a fish, he is hungry again in an hour. If you teach him to catch a fish you do him a good turn."*
> **—ANNE ISABELLA THACKERAY RITCHIE**

As we've discussed, developing your wisdom is a lifelong process. And along the way, the wisdom of others can fuel your learning process. During your FI journey, collecting wisdom from people you trust can be invaluable, but you first need to be receptive to it.

And when you do take the advice and wisdom of others, you should take the next critical step: *understand* their wisdom, don't blindly follow it. Before acting on it, you should make the wisdom "your own" by understanding the decision process that led to their wisdom. Their decision process will teach you a lot more than will their outcome.

LET IT RIDE!

Michael Burry is a physician, investor, and hedge fund manager. In 2000 he founded the hedge fund Scion Capital. When he left his medical practice, he did so with about $40,000 in assets and $145,000 in student loans. As a result, he funded Scion Capital mostly with loans and investments from family and friends.

While Burry's largest investment in 2005 is often expressed in terms of a "bet," it was far from Ashley Revell's bet on red. For starters, his decision to short the housing market (an investment that would only make money if home loans defaulted) began to formulate years earlier, in 2003, as Burry carefully studied the financial markets. Burry eventually homed in on the subprime housing market and its mortgage lending practices.

Over a two-year period, this analysis led him in 2005 to his now-infamous insight: it was not just that housing prices were too high or that borrowers were borrowing too much; he went deeper to recognize that the lenders had lost all restraint and were indiscriminately lending on financial terms that all but assured they would never be repaid. It was financial lunacy! This led to further analysis and his investment thesis that the real estate market (more specifically, the subprime mortgage market) was a bubble that in his estimation would burst sometime in the next three years. Only then did Burry invest, shorting the housing market.

It was a multiyear process to learn all he could about the market, formulate an investment thesis, then stick with it when most people around him (including many Wall Street firms) thought he was bonkers. After shorting mortgages, he continually reevaluated his decision process while the real estate market continued to rise. His investment was losing money (a lot of money) and his investors were getting extremely anxious.

With a bit of irony, Burry later summarized his actions by explaining that he is a "long" investor and generally doesn't look for opportunities to short the market. But his research and deep analysis led him to conclude that in this instance, shorting subprime mortgages was the only logical trade.[38]

Michael Burry's "bet" was not a 20-minute trip to the casino. It took years for his investment to play out. The investment that started as a germ of an idea in 2003 closed out five years later as the housing market collapsed, netting Burry and his investors $800 million.[39]

> *"We never know as much as we'd like to know."*
>
> **—AGATHA CHRISTIE**

In June of 1997 an American journalist, Mary Schmich, wrote a newspaper column in the form of a hypothetical commencement address to graduating students. In it she analogizes the act of giving advice to that of sifting through the disposal for worthwhile tidbits, recycling them, and passing them along. (She goes on, ironically, to dispense invaluable advice that has proven to be of enduring relevance. When you have a few minutes, you should read Schmich's entire *Chicago Tribune* column,[40] or watch this video[41] of it set to the music of Baz Luhrmann):

Her column provided inspiration for this chapter and was the genesis for my proclivity to shy away from giving advice. I much prefer to give information to help you make an informed decision. Everyone's life is different and your personal journey (FI and otherwise) is just that, personal. Learning about managing your money must fit your style and your personality quirks. There is no one-size-fits-all for that.

As I've said before, my goal is to help you with *how* to think about personal finance matters rather than *what* to think. This is why I also don't like to act on others' advice *unless* I've kicked the tires, thought it through, and am willing to accept the counsel as wise *and* appropriate for me. Take responsibility for the decisions you make, regardless of whether the idea originated with you or from the advice of others.

The next time you get a hot stock tip, at the very least figure out if it is based on a Michael Burry–style decision process or based on a friend's sister's boyfriend's second cousin who's got a guy...

Advice can be resplendent with wisdom; it can also impersonate wisdom or be devoid of it. Read, experience, learn...you'll grow to comprehend and separate true wisdom from mediocre advice.

And as you ponder the advice of others, take to heart the old Russian proverb, *Doveryai, no proveryai*, popularized by US President Ronald Reagan when describing negotiations with Russian President Mikhail Gorbachev: "Trust, but verify."

SUGGESTIONS FOR ADDITIONAL READING

Michael Lewis, *The Big Short: Inside the Doomsday Machine* (W.W. Norton & Company, 2010).

9

IT'S ALL IN YOUR HEAD

*"The calm and balanced mind is the strong and great
mind; the hurried and agitated mind is the weak one."*
—WALLACE D. WATTLES

INVESTING IS SO MUCH MORE THAN A NUMBERS GAME. IN CLASSIC
economic theory, decisions are based exclusively on logic and
rational behavior. In the 1970s, behavioral economics began gaining wider acceptance, prominently discussing psychology and
irrational behavior as additional factors impacting financial decision-making.

Behavioral economics has had many notable experiments and
published studies over the years exploring the science and the
psychology of financial decisions. The importance of this field
of study is highlighted by the fact that over the last 30 years, at
least six individuals have earned Nobel Prizes for their work in this
area.[42]

Several books and research papers are dedicated to this topic, but two books in particular have stoked my interest: *Your Money and Your Brain* by Jason Zweig, and *The Psychology of Money* by Morgan Housel. Over the years, I became fascinated with the field of neuro-economics and more broadly behavioral economics.

In the first few pages of his book, Zweig observes that the brain activity of a person making money in the markets is virtually the same as a person "high on cocaine or morphine."[43] Bam! I was hooked. I found that concept to be a profound truth pushing me to learn more about this intriguing discipline at the junction where behavioral sciences and economics converge.

Behavioral economics has shown us that our investing brains oftentimes lead us to make decisions that are illogical, but that make perfect emotional sense. Planning and investing for financial independence requires, by necessity, that you make decisions about an unknown future with unknowable outcomes. As a result, emotions such as hope, greed, jealousy, and FOMO (fear of missing out) can creep into one's decision process.

Behavioral economics is about understanding and harnessing these emotions and keeping them from running amok. It is also about making sure your decision process includes a healthy dose of reasoning mixed in.

I find particularly interesting the number of occasions that we humans show inclinations or have preconceived notions for or against ideas—biases. Psychologists Daniel Kahneman and Amos Tversky famously ran numerous experiments designed to identify biases and explore how emotions impact the mind during the decision-making process. This chapter focuses on cognitive biases—limitations on rational thinking caused by the brain's tendency to perceive information through a filter of personal experiences and preferences.

These cognitive biases can create shortcuts (referred to as heuristics) for the brain to be able to process the vast amount of information it takes in every second. Heuristics ease the cognitive load, making our decision-making process faster and more efficient, but not necessarily more accurate.

FEET DON'T FAIL ME NOW!

A common example of a heuristic is our primal fight-or-flight response to perceived danger. If you're walking at night on a dimly lit street and hear a dog growling ferociously, you can stop and spend precious time letting your brain fully analyze the situation: Is the dog on a leash? Behind a fence? Maybe the dog is all bark and no bite? What are the odds his owner will restrain him? But more likely your fight-or-flight response will intuitively kick in and this mental shortcut gets you the heck out of there before you even realize you're moving. Ferocious dog = get away. That's a valuable heuristic.

Cognitive biases and heuristics, however, are not always helpful. These shortcuts can result in suboptimal decisions that help to explain in part why investor performance often lags the broader market. For the 20-year period ending in 2019, the S&P 500 Index's average return was 6.06%. The average equity fund investor, however, earned a return of only 4.25% (30% less than the market average).[44]

There are several cognitive biases and heuristics that can contribute to this investor performance lag. Not that it is easy to overcome the brain's predisposition to take shortcuts, but recognizing these biases and shortcuts is a step toward improving your decision processes and ultimately your decisions. What follows is a brief discussion of just a few cognitive biases and heuristics that innately play on your investing psyche.

Time Discounting

The importance of being patient. Emotions drive current choices and cost analysis while the analytical parts of the brain focus on the future (distant) benefits. As a result, discretionary spending right now can oftentimes "feel" more valuable to you than investing for some far-off time in the future like retirement.

Unlike casino games of chance, where almost every decision results in immediate consequences (winning money or losing money), long-term investment decisions can take years to reveal their consequences. Invoking your future self can help with decision-making. Remember in Chapter Three where it wasn't obvious that saving an additional $50 could make a meaningful difference? It was your future self that could see that the $50 per month resulted in $100,000 in your FI Portfolio 30 years hence. Projecting out potential future outcomes is a powerful tool in helping you with today's decision and avoiding time discounting.

Greed and the Thrill of the Hunt

The anticipation of a financial gain is intoxicating and the thrill doesn't stop as you imagine the investment just continuing to go up. And ironically, if it goes up as you expected, the thrill wanes even though you made the money you wanted in the first place. As a result, greed can lead investors to continually chase the big payday no matter how bad the odds of success. That's why lottery winners gamble even more after winning—they're hooked on the high of *what if* I can do it one more time!

The neurological "rush" from imagining gains and dreaming up what-if win celebrations is a powerful draw that can force suboptimal decisions. One tool to combat rash decisions is a strategy developed by Suzy Welch, which she refers to as 10/10/10: thinking about decisions in three different time frames.[45] For example:

- How will I feel about the decision 10 minutes from now?

- How about 10 months from now?

- How about 10 years from now?

Or, conversely, how would I feel if I made this decision 10 days ago, 10 months ago, 10 years ago? 10/10/10 helps to level the emotional playing field by giving the future (or past) as much focus and emotional weight as the present.

The Search for Patterns

There is an old saying: "The third time is a trend." Our brains are wired to look for order in chaos. When the brain sees something occur two times in a row, it automatically expects a third time. If a stock's price has increased on two successive days, your brain subconsciously and quite automatically will expect a third day of rising prices.

With minute-to-minute stock market information, flashing green or red indicators can lead you to see patterns where nothing but random data exists. Flash enough info and almost anything can look like a pattern. This can lead unsuspecting investors to believe they have "observed" actionable trends even within the span of a few minutes.

> **NOTE:** High-frequency traders make day traders look like they are standing still. For example, the founder of a high-frequency trading firm, Tradebot, told a group of students in 2008 that his firm's average holding period for stocks was 11 seconds![46]

Simply put, if you think the third time's a charm, it's quite likely anything but.

Hindsight and Overconfidence

Ever tell yourself, "I should have seen that coming"? Once we learn what happened, we convince ourselves we saw it coming or should have seen it.

Think back to late March 2020 as the stock market is wracked by the COVID-19 pandemic and suffers its steepest and fastest decline in over 30 years. The S&P 500 Index goes from peak to trough in just 16 trading days. How much lower will the pandemic and global shutdown ultimately drive the markets? Where do we go from here? Hang on to your wallet. The angst is palpable.

Fast-forward and as of this writing, the S&P 500 Index has more than doubled from its March 2020 low. I'm willing to bet you've had some recent thoughts like, "I **knew** stocks were cheap back then. I should have bought more." This hindsight bias makes you feel less ignorant about the past while doing nothing to correct your ignorance going forward.

The *20th Annual Transamerica Retirement Survey*[47] was published in December 2020. Three-quarters of surveyed workers reported they are saving for retirement and 70% said they are "very or somewhat confident" that they will have enough money to live comfortably in retirement. Yet, when asked about actual dollars saved, 40% of respondents have saved less than $50,000 (with 25% of this subset having saved nothing).

Another study, the *2020 Retirement Confidence Survey*, had similar results regarding confidence levels around having sufficient monthly income in retirement. One-quarter of *retirees* reported that they need at least $1 million in their FI Portfolio, yet 6 out of 10 *workers* have never even attempted to calculate the actual dollar amount needed.[48] The majority of workers assume they will be okay but they don't bother to prove it.

Optimism

The authors of the study *Positive Illusions and Forecasting Errors in Mutual Fund Investment Decisions* found that most participants had consistently overestimated the future performance of their investments. But what I found truly surprising is that participants also overestimated the *past* performance of their investments.[49] Past performance is a known certainty if you simply look at the hard data. Yet most investors when recalling past performance rely less on facts and more on colored memories. In fact, more than a third who believed that they had beaten the market had actually underperformed by at least 5%, and a fourth lagged by at least 15%.[50]

We all tend to inflate our self-assessment. We rationalize that past investment successes are a result of skill, while past failures are attributed to bad luck. We are better than the average investor! But by definition, 50% of investors must be below average—just not us; must be the other guys.

Unfortunately, it seems that a lot of investors would rather go through life blissfully unaware of their incompetence rather than put in the effort to educate themselves on the science and psychology of investing.

Familiarity Breeds
Contentment—and Shortcuts

Peter Lynch (legendary manager of Fidelity's flagship, the Magellan Fund, from 1977 to 1990) is often remembered for offering up the concept of "buy what you know." This was understood by many to mean that if you like a company's products or services, then buy the company's stock.

Lynch, however, never actually said this. What he does suggest throughout his book *One Up on Wall Street* is that liking a company's products or services may be a good reason to become *interested* in a company, but you should never *invest* in a company until you have done your research and due diligence around the potential investment's financial prospects. Sorry, "buy what you know" sounds so much easier.

Children learn early on that the shortest distance between two points is a straight line. Similarly, your brain is constantly searching for the shortest path to making a decision, which is why it oftentimes relies on heuristics to get there.

When your brain sees a succinct catchphrase, the default is to believe and follow it. Quick and easy so the brain can move on to the next task. You need to recognize this bias and guard against it.

Most Wall Street maxims, and for that matter Hollywood maxims (can you tell the difference?), are clever and catchy but of minimal value. For example, "Sell in May and go away." "Fear? That's the other guy's problem." "More is never enough." "Cut your losses when prices fall 10%." "Wait for the pullback." "The trend is your friend." "Buy the rumor, sell the news." "Bulls make money, bears make money, pigs get slaughtered." "This time it'll be different." "Lunch is for wimps."

A lot of these are likely familiar to you and easily remembered, but relying on catchphrases to design and execute your FI plan is the equivalent of buying a house based on the color of the front door.

Framing

Let's say you are offered three different investment opportunities. Investment A has a 14% chance of succeeding. Investment B comes with a one-in-seven chance of making money. Investment C has an 86% chance of losing money. How would you prioritize these opportunities? How does each make you feel? If you did just a little more than read the words of the previous few sentences, you should have realized that all three of these investments have an identical probability of success. As a result, the only variable left to talk about is your emotional response. If you're good with one of these three investments, keeping your emotions in check will lead you to understand you should be equally good with all of them.

When evaluating the risks around a decision, it's important to look at not only the probability of being right but also the probability and consequences of being wrong. When formulating a concept or a plan, look at the complete frame.

NO ONE IS AFRAID OF THE DARK
UNTIL THE LIGHTS GO OUT

In the early 1990s an acquaintance of mine, let's call him Billy Ray, was heavily investing in Cisco Systems almost to the exclusion of all else. Cisco's dominance in enterprise networking hardware propelled its stock gains, and Cisco handily beat the market throughout the '90s.

The company's stock price seemingly had nowhere to go but up. Cisco's ascent was so rapid, it was splitting its stock almost every year. After each split the stock price marched higher, quickly exceeding the presplit price. Starting in March of 1991 through March of 2000, Cisco split its stock nine times. One hundred shares in 1991 grew to 28,800 shares in 2000, turning $18 into more than $20,000 per share.

> **NOTE:** In March of 2000, Cisco stock traded above $82 a share, where its market cap reached a staggering $569 billion—surpassing Microsoft as the world's most valuable company and fueling speculation that it could be the first company to reach a $1 trillion valuation.

In the summer of 1999, standing on the beach basking in the sun with a cold Bud Light in his hand, Billy Ray gleefully explained to me that all he needed was a couple more stock splits and his family would be set for life. Eight months later the dot-com bubble flew into the tip of a knife. At its worst, Cisco lost 89% of its value, falling from a price of $82 per share to $9 in less than three years—a loss of over $400 billion, which at the time was the largest decline by a single stock in the market's history.

Billy Ray had a plan, just not a good plan. Billy Ray's numbers were working for him for almost a decade, and all the while his risk profile was shooting through the roof! Then the dot-com bust punched him squarely on the jaw.

Throughout the '90s, Billy Ray's mind was a perfect storm of cognitive biases and heuristics. If he had stepped back to contemplate what could go wrong and weighed the cost of failure, he may have noticed his overconfidence, his concentrated assets and lack of diversification, his whole-hearted belief that the recent past "trend" of stock splits and price increases would continue unabated, etc. As we talked about in Chapter Two, Billy Ray would have been well-served by doing some modeling, "what-if" calculations, risk analysis, and course-correcting. PCR: Plan, Course-Correct, Repeat.

> **NOTE:** The qualitative aspects of a plan need to be continually evaluated, not just the quantitative numbers. You cannot continually undercontribute to your FI Portfolio hoping and praying the stock market will make up the shortfall. "Hope" is not a plan.

It takes hard work to get your FI Portfolio to the point that you no longer have to work hard. That includes recognizing cognitive biases and keeping those biases from clouding your planning process. If you fail to see these reflexive errors that occur in your mind, your mind will simply continue to make them.

Stay focused on balancing (1) the probability that your investment thesis will be successful, with (2) the financial and emotional cost of being wrong. Your journey through Life's Complete Financial Arc will be happier and less stressful. As with most things in life, no one wants to be caught off balance.

SUGGESTIONS FOR ADDITIONAL READING

Jason Zweig, *Your Money and Your Brain: How the New Science of Neuroeconomics Can Help Make You Rich* (Simon & Schuster, 2007).

Morgan Housel, *The Psychology of Money: Timeless Lessons on Wealth, Greed, and Happiness* (Harriman House, 2020).

10

DON'T SPECULATE
ABOUT INVESTING

"There are two times in a man's life when he shouldn't speculate: when he can't afford it and when he can."

—MARK TWAIN

TO BE A SUCCESSFUL INVESTOR, YOU FIRST NEED TO BE AN INVESTOR.

Let's start with gaining a better understanding of speculators and investors, and why people might confuse the two. At a basic level, speculators look at the stock market as a way to "make money" flipping stocks, while investors view it as a way to invest their hard-earned capital to earn a reasonable return over time by owning a piece of an operating business. Sort of like buying a basket of fruit to resell vs. buying fruit trees to enjoy the crop year after year. Going beyond my rudimentary metaphor, here's how a couple of influential money managers who have stood the test of time have differentiated the two.

Benjamin Graham lays out a clear definition of investing and speculating in his seminal book *The Intelligent Investor*. An investment is based on significant research and analysis. Such an investment should also be focused on the safety of your capital as well as a reasonable expectation of profit.[51] Graham goes on to note that, "Outright speculation is neither illegal, immoral, nor (for most people) fattening to the pocketbook. More than that, some speculation is necessary..." since with most stocks there is the real possibility of significant gain or loss "...and the risks therein must be assumed by someone."[52]

Think about the last time you were discussing a particular stock over drinks, or while getting your hair cut. Was the conversation centered on the business's products, long-term profit potential, and quality of management, or was the conversation focused on whether the price of the stock was going to go up or down over the next few days/ weeks/months? During that conversation, did you learn anything about the company beyond the letters of its ticker symbol?

In his 1991 book, *Margin of Safety*, Seth Klarman, CEO and portfolio manager of the $30 billion Baupost Group hedge fund, amplifies Graham's definition by homing in on investment fundamentals. He notes that over the long term, investors understand that stock prices will eventually track a company's underlying business fundamentals. Speculators, on the other hand, will buy a stock solely because they think its stock price will increase, or conversely, sell a stock because they believe the stock price will decrease (regardless of fundamentals).[53]

Graham, Klarman, Buffett, and countless others suggest unequivocally that if you want to put your money in the markets it is of the utmost importance that you use your hard-earned cash to "invest," not "speculate"—and that you thoroughly appreciate the difference.

> *"Investors should purchase stocks like they purchase groceries, not like they purchase perfume."*
> **—BENJAMIN GRAHAM**

Part of the struggle with differentiating speculators and investors is that they share certain traits (e.g., buying and selling stocks), so the line between them can be blurry. Let's take a closer look at this common ground and see where they begin to diverge.

Trading volume is a good place to start. Speculating oftentimes includes more frequent trading of stocks (relative to investors). Day-to-day share price fluctuations are generally of little consequence unless an investor wants to—or is forced to—trade. Speculators relish such price movements.

With stock tickers easily accessible to anyone with a smartphone, discount brokers offering commission-free trading, and 24-hour "news" channels dedicated to stocks, it's easy to understand the draw of (or push toward) trading, including day-trading.

Indicative of increasing trading levels, the following chart summarizes the average holding period for all stocks on the New York Stock Exchange (including institutional investors as well as retail (individual) investors):

Shrinking Times

— Holding Period of Stocks in Years

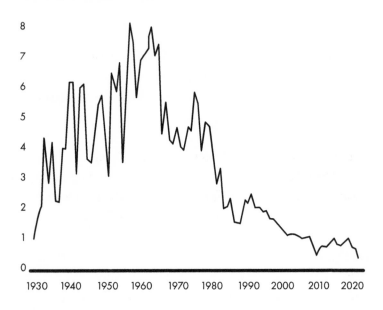

Source: Reuters[54]

During the 1950s and '60s, the average stock was held for more than seven years. By the 1980s the average was down to less than three years, and by the turn of the millennium through today it has fallen to less than one year. Reuters noted that by June 2020 the average holding period had declined to just five and a half months. While not a direct indicator of increased speculation, I would argue that company fundamentals don't fluctuate nearly as often or as widely as stocks trade, especially day to day.

Regardless of whether speculation is the cause, when it comes to the frequency of stock trades in a portfolio (referred to as "turnover") several studies have found a negative correlation with returns. A 2019 study examined a database of 46,000 mutual funds for the period 2000–2016. Across *all* equity fund categories, the funds with higher turnover earned lower returns.[55] The data is clear: the more trading you do (a hallmark of most speculators), the higher your transaction costs, and consequently the lower your returns.

PRICE AND VALUE ARE TWO FACTORS, NOT ONE

A lot of people think they make money when they sell a stock. But successful investors know they make their money when they buy a quality company at the right price. Choosing a good company is half the equation. You need to invest in a good company *at a reasonable price*. No matter how "good" a company is, if you over-pay for it, your profit potential is reduced, or worse, eliminated.

We all know this rudimentary rule of investing: buy low, sell high. Many speculators, however, get caught doing just the opposite, buying high and selling low because they use price movement as their sole indicator to buy or sell. Stocks that are moving up in price, especially in "hot" or trendy industries, often attract buyers, driving prices up.

People get excited with all the "news" and don't want to be left on the sideline filled with FOMO. They jump into a stock that's already been bid up and is trading at premium, betting they can flip it for a profit.

The fundamental problem with buying an expensive or overpriced security is a too-common consequence of the Greater Fool Theory. The theory posits that the price of a stock is not determined by its intrinsic value but rather by supply and demand regardless of quality. Simply stated, you can make money speculating on future prices because there will *always* be an irrational buyer ("greater fool") who will be willing to pay more than you paid, even if you paid too much.

Greater fools do exist, but can you count on them to show up when you need them most? Bottom line, I don't know what the market is going to do and neither does anyone else. Trying to predict the short-term direction of the market is futile. Think dot-com bubble, the Financial Crisis, the COVID-19-induced drop, or for a much older historical perspective, tulip mania.[56] The theory works right up until it doesn't.

All successful businesses will eventually produce cash flow for the benefit of their shareholders (evidenced by growing dividends, stock buybacks, increased earnings leading to higher stock valuations, etc.). Speculation, on the other hand, depends solely on future price movements regardless of underlying fundamentals. As a result, the more of your financial assets you deploy in speculative pursuits, the more of your long-term returns you are likely sacrificing in pursuit of the elusive quick buck.

DO YOU WANT TO BET ON IT?

Annie Duke is a former professional poker player, winning more than $4 million in tournament poker. She was also awarded a National Science Foundation Fellowship to study cognitive psychology at the University of Pennsylvania. In 2018, she authored her national bestselling book, *Thinking in Bets: Making*

Smarter Decisions When You Don't Have All the Facts. Her book is a fascinating exploration of probabilistic thinking and rational decision-making.

Duke begins with expanding our understanding of betting. When we think of betting, most of us conjure up images of casinos, lottery tickets, and gambling on sports. But let's view betting through a wide-angle lens. A "bet" also includes making a probabilistic choice about whether something will happen or not. With this broader definition, we see that picking a number on the roulette wheel and deciding if you should take your umbrella are both "bets." Both are choices about the future: what are the chances the ball lands on your number, or the chance that the clouds will bring rain?

Probabilistic thinking explores the concept that every decision involves a "bet" on an unknown future. Even if you know every fact there is to know about an investment (as improbable as that may be), you still can't know "facts" that have yet to occur. The future is unknown and unknowable. As we discussed in previous chapters, you use all the information you have available to you to make an informed decision about an uncertain future, giving yourself the best chance at a successful outcome. But it's just that, a *chance*.

Speculators are often compared to gamblers in that they are "betting" on whether stock prices will go up or down in the near term. If speculators are making bets, what are investors doing? If you have digested the preceding few paragraphs, then you know that, ironically, investors are making bets too.

Having weighed the relative probabilities, knowing we don't know everything and that lady luck may or may not show up, we "bet" on a *probable* (and uncertain) future outcome and make our investment choice. As such, speculators and investors have "betting" in common. Now, the key distinction begins to emerge: the level of effort put into evaluating the bet.

"Anytime you have a 50/50 chance of getting something right, there's a 90% probability you'll get it wrong."

—ANDY ROONEY

Since every decision you make has some level of uncertainty, the challenge successful investors take on is how to weigh the alternatives. Enter the world of probabilities.

Just like in the game of blackjack, you should make the bet only if the odds are in your favor. Unlike blackjack, however, where decisions are routinely processed and made in a matter of seconds, investors have the luxury of more time to step back and cogitate on the opportunity. The thought process may be the same, but don't speed through the investment decision as if you're sitting at the blackjack table.

Let's look at a simple example. Alex is presented with an opportunity to invest $1,000 that if successful will earn him $10,000. Adriana is presented the same opportunity but she digs a little deeper and estimates that there is a 10% probability of earning the $10,000 and a 90% probability that she will lose her $1,000. Both have *a chance* at a successful outcome, but as more facts see the light of day, the evaluation tips in one direction over the other. What if there is no sunlight? Get a strong flashlight or move on and look for another opportunity.

> *"The happiness of your life depends on the quality of your thoughts."*
>
> **—MARCUS AURELIUS**

In the early days of November 2016, the *New York Times* predicted that Hillary Clinton had an 85% chance of winning the US presidency.[57] (Most news outlets had similar predictions.) When Donald Trump won, people were quick to point out that the political commentators got it wrong. But the commentators never said Clinton *will* win. In fact, the *Times* implicitly said that there was a 15% chance she would lose—and she did lose.

When judging others, it's easier to choose between right and wrong than to analyze the opinion on a probability basis. No need to give it much thought. Right or wrong—that's it. But most of our financial decisions are not so binary.

When you get away from thinking in absolutes, 100% right or 100% wrong, and start thinking in probabilities, you begin to contextualize the decision at hand. As a result, your decision process improves because your decisions are no longer simply about black or white, "but about calibrating among all the shades of grey."[58]

If you're acting on the investment advice of others, ask them for their level of confidence, expressed as a percentage. If they tell you 100%—well, that's a "guarantee" that no one can deliver; walk away from it. When they give you an honest answer of something less than 100%, let's say they are 80% confident, then your next question is asking about the 20%, i.e., what could go wrong. This should lead to a more informed, balanced dialogue as you evaluate the opportunity.

> **NOTE:** Weather forecasters give their weather predictions hand in hand with their level of confidence in that prediction, e.g., 75% chance of rain—you make your decision accordingly. Similarly, doctors will express their level of confidence in a procedure, e.g., 99 out of 100 patients find the procedure to be helpful—and you make your decision. When making investment recommendations, why is it that financial pundits don't routinely express their level of confidence—or lack thereof?

Since we can't "guarantee" a good outcome (after all, the future is unknown), making better-informed decisions is about evaluating and increasing our odds of a good outcome, which moves us toward investing and away from speculating.

> *"One of the funny things about the stock market is that every time one person buys, another sells, and both think they are astute."*
>
> **—WILLIAM FEATHER**

When the market is crashing down, headlines are quick to point out that people are dumping stocks and "everyone" is selling. If this were true, the market would literally come to a screeching halt. What the pundits fail to mention is that for "everyone" to be selling, someone must be buying.

Trading volume is not indicative of "selling" activity alone. For every seller in the stock market, there is a buyer. That's how the markets work. When the market averages are dramatically dropping ("crashing") it simply means that sellers are continually lowering the prices at which they are willing to sell and buyers are lowering the prices at which they are willing to buy. (When market averages are rising, the opposite is true.)

On March 23, 2020, when the S&P 500 hit its 10-year low, 7.4 billion shares of stock were sold that day...and bought that day!

Speculators seek to capitalize on the trajectory of these price moves. In contrast, investors are trying to calibrate how much of the selling is based on fear (potentially indicating a discount to the company's intrinsic value) and how much of the buying is based on greed (or potential premium over value). This is true whether the market is going up or down, and whether we are talking about an individual company or the market as a whole.

The market would be much easier to navigate if trading was based solely on company fundamentals, but emotions can and do weigh heavily on investors' and speculators' minds, which impacts prices and increases trading levels. Every day the market is filled with people trading fear and greed back and forth between each other. In turn, unchecked emotions can transform purported investment actions into speculations.

"Think for yourself or others will think for you without thinking of you."

—HENRY DAVID THOREAU

Why does it even matter that we understand the distinction between speculating and investing? Self-awareness. So that you don't walk out onto the grass and get hit in the head with a baseball because you thought you were playing golf. As Benjamin Graham warns us in *The Intelligent Investor*, the most "unintelligent" thing you can do is "speculating when you think you are investing" since the resulting loss could knock you on your butt and scare you right out of the market altogether.

The lure of speculating is powerful, just as can be the pull of a casino or a sports wager. If you want to try your luck at it, set aside a small amount of your capital—the less the better, but never more than 10% of your portfolio—and never mingle it with your FI Portfolio. Use a separate brokerage account. And if you happen to lose it all, rather than contributing more money to it, I would recommend closing the account for good.

To paraphrase Winston Churchill: you can always count on investors to do the right thing—after they have tried everything else.

> "The best time to plant a tree is twenty years ago. The second-best time is today."
>
> **—CHINESE PROVERB**

During the Gilded Age of the late 19th century, the Vanderbilts were one of America's wealthiest families. The family fortune blossomed under the direction of Cornelius Vanderbilt, who had the foresight and boldness to invest in a cross-country railway system that made possible transcontinental travel and commerce on a grand scale. In developing a symbol of the Vanderbilt family's values for the family crest, they chose to include oak leaves and acorns. Nuts; why nuts? The Vanderbilts knew that an acorn, when planted and nurtured, would slowly but inevitably grow into a mighty oak tree providing shade, a source of wood, and yes, more acorns for generations to come. Treat your stock investments as future oak trees, not tulips.

> **NOTE:** If you have the chance to visit and tour the Vanderbilts' summer cottage, the Breakers, in Newport, Rhode Island, make note of the acorn symbolism throughout the property, embedded in several ornate gilded ornaments.

A successful investor has an intellectual curiosity and an unwavering work ethic. Success comes from working hard, not hardly working.

Your position on the speculator–investor spectrum is up to you. Just be sure to recognize two things: (1) attitudes can covertly change from opportunity to opportunity; and (2) you need to know whether to show up with a nine iron or a baseball bat.

Think back to Chapter Eight. Do you want to "bet" like Ashley Revell on roulette, or "bet" like Michael Burry on the housing market? I know whom I prefer to emulate when I grow up—how about you?

SUGGESTIONS FOR ADDITIONAL READING

Annie Duke, *Thinking in Bets: Making Smarter Decisions When You Don't Have All the Facts* (Penguin Publishing Group, 2018).

Michael J. Mauboussin, *The Success Equation: Untangling Skill and Luck in Business, Sports, and Investing* (Harvard Business Review Press, 2012).

Benjamin Graham, *The Intelligent Investor: The Definitive Book on Value Investing* with commentary by Jason Zweig (in particular, Chapters 8 and 20) (HarperCollins, 2003).

Burton G. Malkiel, *A Random Walk Down Wall Street: The Time-Tested Strategy for Successful Investing* (W. W. Norton & Company, 2019).

11

HISTORY TEACHES, BUT DO WE LEARN?—PART I

"History doesn't repeat itself but it often rhymes."

—MARK TWAIN

GLOBAL STOCK MARKETS HAVE BEEN AROUND FOR HUNDREDS OF years. The companies change, the products and services evolve, but broad market fundamentals (as opposed to individual companies) are remarkably consistent over the millennia. And just as importantly, the actions and reactions of market participants are eerily similar even as time and evolution march on.

As a result, every successful investor I know is a student of the financial markets. Understanding the past coupled with a firm grasp on investor psychology provides investors with foundational knowledge that can help improve investment decisions and financial planning. Knowing where we have been can provide clues to where we might be going. We can learn from those who came before us and maybe, just maybe, avoid some big mistakes. To quote Harry S. Truman, "There is nothing new in the world, except the history you do not know." I find Truman's observation to be quite insightful when discussing the financial markets.

CHANGE IS INEVITABLE
AND ACCELERATING

Since the inception of the Dow Jones Industrial Average Index (DJIA) in 1896, not one company has consistently remained a component of the Average. Since 1928, when the DJIA was expanded to include its present-day total of 30 companies, 67 changes have occurred.

> **NOTE:** General Electric was an original component, dropped out briefly, and since 1907 had been a continuous member of the Average. But alas, it too succumbed to the winds of change. In 2018, after more than 110 years, GE was dropped and replaced by Walgreens Boots Alliance.

Similarly, turnover in the S&P 500 Index is currently around 5% per year. Said another way, the average company will have nowhere near GE's longevity, spending less than 20 years as a component of the Index. If we look at the largest companies in the Index (as of late 2021), the top 10 companies make up over 28% of the value of the Index, but only one of them (Microsoft) was in the top 10 in

2000. Six out of the 10 weren't even among the 500 companies in the entire Index in 2000. One study noted that in 1964, the average tenure of companies in the S&P 500 was 33 years. By 2016 tenure narrowed to 24 years, and it is forecasted to shrink to 15–20 years this decade.[59]

While talk around individual companies can be exciting, a broader view of the history of markets is more instructive. An in-depth analysis of hundreds of years of market history is well beyond the scope of this book, but one aspect worth exploring is the recurring cycles of boom and bust. These cycles have played out repeatedly with striking similarities. Let's look at just a handful of historical periods from the last 100 years and see what recurring themes we can glean from them.

The Roaring '20s (That Is, the 1920s)

The stock market during the early 20th century was booming on the back of innovations including the automobile, penicillin, the refrigerator, frozen foods, etc., and financial innovations such as buying stocks "on margin." During the 1920s, many speculators were buying stocks by putting down only 10–20% of the cost in cash and borrowing the remaining 80–90%.

With easy access to margin debt and stories of fortunes being made, the stock market opened up to millions of new investors. On top of all that debt, the stock market of that time was not highly regulated, allowing unbridled speculation and even fraud to run wild. From 1921 to mid-1929 the stock market rose 500%. There seemed to be no end in sight for the booming economy, rising stock prices, and investor exuberance.

After nearly a decade of economic growth and expansion, Yale economist Irving Fisher, in early October 1929, famously declared that "stock prices have reached what looks like a permanently high plateau." Just a few short weeks after Fisher's comment, on Thursday, October 24, 1929, the stock market crash of 1929 began, triggering the Great Depression. The following Monday, the DJIA plunged 13% and was followed up on Tuesday, October 29, with another precipitous 12% drop, sending shock waves across global financial markets. For the next few months, however, the market rebounded quite nicely and by April 1930 reached a level within 2% of where the market was at the beginning of 1929.

Just when investors thought they saw the light at the end of the tunnel they slowly realized it was, as Robert Lowell once quipped, the headlamp of an oncoming train. The market went into a free fall that lasted two years. Just like that initial rebound, the two-year period was filled with mini bounces but those were incessantly followed by larger downward movements. At the bottom, in July 1932, the market had fallen 90% from its 1929 high point.

Lessons learned from the Great Depression resulted in the creation of new financial infrastructure in America. Several new pieces of legislation, most of which are still in effect today, offered safeguards to investors and the markets. The Securities Act of 1933 made the stock issuance process and a company's financial statements more transparent; the Securities Exchange Act of 1934 governs the buying and selling of securities and also empowered the US Securities and Exchange Commission (SEC); and the Investment Company Act of 1940 regulates the mutual fund industry and laid the groundwork for the asset management industry. The Glass-Steagall Act of 1933 separated investment banking from retail banking; among other things, it prohibited investment banks from having a controlling interest in retail banks and prohibited retail banks from using depositors' funds for risky investments.

Glass-Steagall, along with FDIC insurance, restored faith in retail banks with investors knowing their deposits could only be invested in low-risk securities. This was the law of the land for almost seven decades. But by the late 1990s, attitudes began to change. The Great Depression was a distant memory of a prior generation's problem. Banks had convinced enough folks that Glass-Steagall restricted them too much and they couldn't compete with foreign firms that could invest more aggressively and therefore offer higher returns to investors. As a result, the Financial Services Modernization Act in 1999 repealed Glass-Steagall.

Less than 10 years after the Glass-Steagall repeal, some of the banks that had put retail and investment activities back together under one umbrella became "too big to fail." This contributed, at least in part, to the 2008–2009 financial crisis and a federal government bailout to avoid another depression.

With excruciating pain, we had to relearn the reasons that we passed the Glass-Steagall Act in the first place.

> **NOTE:** With a bit of irony, by 2015 the Dodd-Frank Wall Street Reform and Consumer Protection Act essentially reinstated a few, but not all, of Glass-Steagall's provisions.

History can tell us a lot if we are willing to listen. Now, if we could just learn to listen *before* taking action.

The Electronics Boom

In the late 1950s, the Space Race was not only a scientific endeavor that captured the imagination of millions, but it also ignited a liftoff of electronics stocks on Wall Street. Companies with some variation of the word "electronics" in their name found speculators eager to bid up the price of their stock, regardless of whether the company had anything to do with the electronics industry. Names that included "tronics," "sonics," or "tron" were particularly attractive. Princeton Professor Burton G. Malkiel writes: "There were a host of 'trons' such as Astron, Dutron, Vulcatron, and Transitron, and a number of 'onics' such as Circuitronics, Supronics, Videotronics, and several Electrosonics companies." Not to be outdone, someone came up with "the winning combination of Powertron Ultrasonics."[60]

Investors were valuing these companies not based on company fundamentals but on the promise of this "new era" economy. A 1999 *Forbes* article noted that promoters arrived on the scene to create interest in these companies and, as a result, stock multiples rose to astronomical levels of 50, 100, or even 200 times earnings.[61]

Existing companies didn't want to be left out in the cold, so some changed their name to try and cash in on the electronics and Space Race boom. For example, American Music Guild, which sold record players door to door, changed its name to Space-Tone, then sold shares in an IPO at $2 and within weeks saw its stock price increase 600%.[62]

By 1962, the euphoria around the "tronics" companies withered on the vine and their stock valuations shriveled up as the DJIA slid

27%. In fact, 1962 was the worst year for the DJIA since 1931, the height of the Great Depression.

The Nifty Fifty

On the back of the electronics boom and bust, investors turned to a group of growth stocks that were viewed as stable, reliable long-term investments (often described as "one-decision stocks," implying you could buy and simply hold them forever). During the second half of the 1960s and early 1970s, the list of these 50 blue-chip companies included the likes of General Electric, IBM, Texas Instruments, Digital Equipment, Polaroid, Xerox, McDonald's, and Avon Products. All had large market caps with consistent earnings growth and ever-increasing P/E multiples. (P/E is a ratio of a company's stock price to its earnings per share.)

Investing in this group of large companies, by institutional investors and individuals alike, helped drive the bull market. Investors became enamored with "growth at any price," leaving behind the focus on a company's fundamentals and believing that one could count on continuing earnings growth indefinitely. As a result, no price seemed too high to pay for these stocks. In 1972, the average P/E for the Nifty Fifty was 42 times earnings while the average for the entire S&P 500 was less than half that at 19 times earnings. Among the high end of the group, McDonald's was trading at 83 times earnings, Avon at 61 times earnings, and Polaroid at a lofty 95 times earnings.

In early 1973, amid slowing economic growth and rising inflation, the stock market began to slide downward. Then the OPEC oil embargo and the Watergate scandal (that led to President Richard Nixon's resignation) punctuated what became the second-longest bear market in history—second only to the Great Depression. The 21-month-long bear market of 1973–1974, which saw the S&P 500 lose 42% of its value, brought most of these high fliers down with it. McDonald's stock price dropped 70%, Avon dropped more than 85%, and Polaroid plummeted 90%.

With hindsight, some of the Nifty Fifty eventually provided solid *long-term* investment returns, but it would require significant investor patience and years if not decades to reap those returns, all while others in the Nifty Fifty would flirt with bankruptcy and/or flame out completely.

The Dot-Com Bubble

The dot-com bubble, also known as the internet bubble, was a rapid rise in technology stock valuations that drove the bull market during the 1990s. Like the electronics boom, it was fueled by entrepreneurs and speculators looking to capitalize on a burgeoning and relatively new technology, the internet. In January of 1992, the technology-heavy Nasdaq Composite Index was at a level of 580. In March 2000, it peaked at 5,100, an almost ninefold increase of 879% in less than nine years.

Internet companies were forming at a rapid pace and quickly selling shares through IPOs. Stock prices were then bid up and up thanks to the excitement and promise that this new technology and industry appeared to deliver. During 1999–2000, 892 companies had IPOs in the United States; a majority were technology-related.

That's an average of two new companies every single trading day for two straight years.

One of the earliest of the large internet companies was theGlobe.com (a nascent social media site that planned to make money from advertisers). Its IPO was on November 13, 1998, with the initial offering price set at $9 per share. On its first day of trading, the stock rocketed up 977% to $97 before pulling back and closing the day up "only" 605% at $63.50. Speculators didn't seem to mind that although theGlobe.com had a plan to make money, it had no actual revenue.

During the internet craze, an investment banker quipped to me that it was good if a potential IPO company was not profitable and even better if it had zero revenue. That way, it can't be evaluated on traditional fundamental benchmarks, such as earnings per share, revenue per share, etc., and consequently can be bestowed with a lofty "internet valuation."

The promise of a "great idea" and a compelling story, coupled with no underlying fundamentals, was the roadmap to selling stock to the investing public at excessively high valuations, and raising large amounts of capital for the company. It worked and the rush was on.

Anyone with an idea on the back of a cocktail napkin and a cool company name, which usually included ".com," could seemingly sell shares at will and grab money from eager speculators. In short order we saw Flooz.com, Pets.com, DrugStore.com, Garden.com, Webvan.com, and eToys.com, to name just a few of the hundreds of companies that were born during the craze.

> *"That which we call a rose by any other name would smell as sweet."*
>
> **—WILLIAM SHAKESPEARE**

What's in a name? Apparently, a lot. A 2001 study by a group of Purdue University researchers found that 95 existing companies that rebranded by adding ".com," ".net," or "internet" to their names saw their share price increase by an average of 74% in the 10 days surrounding the announcement day. Ten of the companies had a core business that was not even internet-related.[63]

My personal favorite, Kozmo.com (no relation), didn't even make it to its planned IPO. It was founded in 1998 and quickly raised $250 million from private investors (including $60 million from Amazon) on the promise of a one-hour internet-based delivery service for small purchases. Kozmo.com couldn't deliver (pun intended). It had burned through all its cash and closed up shop in early 2001, just three years after its founding.

Not all dot-coms failed but all took a hit as the bubble burst and the Nasdaq fell almost 80% over the ensuing two years to a low in October of 2002. Those dot-coms that adapted, refocused on core business fundamentals, and delivered quality products and services not only survived but continue to thrive today (e.g., Amazon, eBay). But for every company that managed to carry on, dozens of others like Kozmo.com and eToys.com imploded and filled the dot-com graveyard, wiping out some $5 trillion in market capitalization from the Nasdaq's peak.

NOTE: After the internet bubble bust of the early 2000s, companies were again similarly quick to change names–this time by *dropping* the dot-com moniker and the negative stigma it had come to convey. A prime example: in 1998, Mecklermedia changed its name to Internet.com. Three years later, Internet.com became INTMedia Group with its CEO pointing out, "It's window dressing for the financial community." On the news of this second name change, the company's stock price jumped 54%.[64]

The dot-com era was among the earliest bubbles that I personally experienced during my formative investing years. (Unfortunately, I had not yet studied the market's previous bubbles.) What a ride it was. I recall on several Fridays sitting with my friend Steve, counting our riches while lamenting the fact that our dot-com stock pick du jour was up "only" 25% for the *week*. Or that our IPO stock had "only" quadrupled in the month since it went public. We laughed and we fantasized a lot about our imminent fortunes.

Where did all that speculative trading and all those paper gains get me? Nowhere fast. I gave it all back (and then some) as the bubble burst and the Nasdaq fell incessantly for two years. Mercifully, I had digested at least one other lesson prior to this crash: don't put all your eggs in one basket—the majority of my FI Portfolio survived and would soldier on!

This technology, the internet, was and is a "change the world" technological advancement. But like the technology innovations that came before it, not all companies or investors early to the party are the ones who achieve long-term gains. So even if you had the foresight to identify this tech as "game-changing," you would have still been faced with the daunting task of identifying the select list of those companies that would prosper with your investment—eToys.com anyone?

> **NOTE:** Being late to the party isn't necessarily a bad thing. Some second-generation internet companies that followed the bust—for example, Google, Meta (f.k.a. Facebook), and YouTube—were able to leverage the infrastructure built during the dot-com period and scale up their businesses at unprecedented speed.

Cryptocurrency and Blockchain

Blockchain is a distributed-ledger technology that was developed in 2008 to serve as the transaction ledger of the cryptocurrency Bitcoin. Cryptocurrencies and, more broadly, blockchain technology garnered significant interest. And as we've seen before, the excitement around a new technology can sometimes escalate to mania and lead to financial bubbles.

Although not on the scale of the dot-com bubble, the blockchain frenzy was no less dramatic. For me, one company epitomized the irrational euphoria that can drive markets to bubble levels. In December of 2017, the popular nonalcoholic beverage maker Long Island Iced Tea Company announced that it was shifting its primary focus toward the exploration of and investment in opportunities that leverage the benefits of blockchain technology. The company also noted that it was changing its name to Long Blockchain Corp. On the next trading day following the announcement, the stock price skyrocketed 432% even though Long Blockchain had not yet invested in or partnered with any companies involved with blockchain technology.[65]

Long Blockchain Corp. wasn't alone in trying to capitalize on this new technology and wasn't even the first beverage company to try it. A Hong Kong company, SkyPeople Fruit Juice, had a few months earlier changed its name to Future FinTech and saw its stock price jump 200%. A UK company, Online PLC, saw its stock price jump 394% after announcing a plan to insert one word into its name and become Online Blockchain PLC.[66]

Another UK firm, Stapleton Capital (without any reported revenues), saw its stock price double after it changed its name to Blockchain Worldwide and announced plans to make acquisitions within the blockchain technology industry.

A vaping company, California-based Vapetek Inc., decided to change its name to Nodechain Inc., and another tea maker in Hong Kong, Ping Shan Tea Group Limited, rebranded itself as Blockchain Group Co. Ltd.

Unlike the dot-com bubble that took years to deflate, it only took a few months for the speculative mania surrounding blockchain to come crashing down. For the most part, stock prices for these and similar companies came down to earth by the spring of 2018, and for Long Blockchain it only got worse from there. Long Blockchain was delisted from the Nasdaq stock market and was investigated by the SEC and separately by the FBI, which alleged insider trading and securities fraud.[67]

Blockchain is still a promising technology, but, just as the bubbles that came before, investors need to remain mindful of company fundamentals, and cautious of blindly following a fluffy narrative and the crowd to dizzying heights.

"If an ass goes traveling, he will not come home a horse."
—THOMAS FULLER

If you think that no one these days is swayed by a name, look at this sample list of catchy (and quite real) ticker symbols that issuers have scrambled to dream up for their funds. (Who can be bothered with remembering actual fund names?):

- FOMO (Tuttle Capital Management's the Fear of Missing Out ETF): leveraging the retail trading boom by investing in trendy "meme stocks." And what a fun name, FOMO, to repeatedly throw around at parties.

- BUZZ (VanEck Vectors Social Sentiment ETF): invests in stocks with "the most bullish investor sentiment and perception"—for whatever that tells you about the long term.

- MOON (Direxion Moonshot Innovators ETF): invests in 50 companies "deemed to have the highest early-stage composite innovation scores."

- FAD (First Trust Multi Cap Growth AlphaDEX ETF): it's been around since 2007 so despite its ticker, it appears to have some measure of longevity.

- TAN (Invesco Solar ETF): who doesn't enjoy a day in the sun?

- FATT (Tuttle Capital Management's Fat Tail Risk ETF): "Designed to offer positive carry tail risk." Not to be confused with Funny at the Time, Friday at the Track, or Fitz and the Tantrums.

NOTE: By the way, the range of expenses for these funds is 0.6% to 1.15%, which is 20-40 times higher than a run-of-the-mill index fund like Vanguard's Total Stock Market ETF (VTI) at 0.03%. It seems that owning shares of a fund with a catchy ticker symbol does not come cheap.

Another recently trending industry, cloud computing, has seen a plethora of companies trying to cash in on this hot market with names such as Spectro Cloud, Standing Cloud, Tower Cloud, JumpCloud, Cloudant, CloudBolt, CloudShare, Cloud Source, and CloudHealth. It's getting cloudy out there. (Sorry, I couldn't resist the pun.)

Like catchphrases, memorable ticker symbols and company names are just that—memorable. Nothing more, nothing less. By design they are likable and catch your attention, but that does not circumvent the need for you to do your homework before investing.

"The four most expensive words in the English language are, 'This time it's different.'"

—SIR JOHN TEMPLETON

All the boom-and-bust cycles have a few recurring ingredients: a compelling story around a new and exciting "change the world" industry or idea; investors' excessive use of margin (debt) to amplify their investments; the next generation of speculators looking for the big score and believing the hyped but unproven growth potential; and most speculators (young and old) ignoring, or ignorant of, past lessons.

What lessons? (1) The price you pay does matter. You can pay too much even for a "good" company. (2) Trees don't reach the sky. A company cannot grow at an ever-accelerating rate, and its growth will not go on forever. (3) Debt doesn't disappear. Lenders want to be paid back even when the cash was used to buy stocks that did evaporate. (4) Gravity wins. Reversion to the mean inevitably pulls prices toward their long-term trend line.

And more disturbing than the repetition of the same mistakes is the shortening of the time between such follies. The "electronics" boom came some 30 years after the Great Depression, followed by the Nifty Fifty some 15 years later and the dot-com bust again 15 years later, followed by the housing bubble and financial crisis nine years later. And then nine years after the housing-induced collapse of the market, the blockchain bubble deflated. The "greater fool theory" raises its head on a grand scale with what appears to be increasing frequency.

"Learn every day, but especially from the experiences of others—it's cheaper."

—JACK BOGLE

Whether you are a passive index investor or an individual stock picker, understanding historical lessons can help you avoid surprises and minimize rash decisions as the next (inevitable) boom-and-bust cycle runs its course.

There are no good or bad stocks, just correctly or incorrectly priced ones. Successful investing entails the study of those relative pricing differences.

Investors can become successful investors, but most often only after they have learned about, or experienced firsthand, the foot faults of others.

Sir John Templeton's famous warning about the potential danger in the concept that "this time it's different" does not mean that the times are *never* different. In fact, Templeton conceded that when people make the case, 20% of the time they are right.[68] The problems, however, often arise when people think those differences will go on, unabated, forever. The economic landscape shifts, prospects evolve, sentiments change direction, and as a result, the broader boom-and-bust cycles have consistently turned up.

"How do you go bankrupt? Two ways. Gradually, then suddenly."

—ERNEST HEMINGWAY

You may view the above summary of boom-and-bust cycles as instructive or mildly curious anecdotes. Either way, know this: reading about lost money does not come close to stirring up the emotions of actually losing money. Losing a chunk of hard-earned cash that you once held in your brokerage account—oh, that's a feeling you won't want to rekindle.

You need to understand the current landscape and monitor changes that might impact the future. Of equal importance, do not forget or unlearn the lessons history has taught us.

SUGGESTIONS FOR ADDITIONAL READING

Brent Goldfarb and David Kirsch, *Bubbles and Crashes: The Boom and Bust of Technological Innovation* (Stanford University Press, 2019).

Ben Carlson, *Don't Fall for It: A Short History of Financial Scams* (John Wiley & Sons, 2020).

William J. Bernstein, *The Delusions of Crowds: Why People Go Mad in Groups* (Grove/Atlantic, 2021).

12

HISTORY TEACHES, BUT DO WE LEARN?— PART II

"I can calculate the motion of the heavenly bodies, but not the madness in people."

—ISAAC NEWTON

ALMOST EVERY MODERN-DAY INVESTMENT FOR SALE TO THE PUBLIC comes with a version of the following disclaimer (based on SEC Rule 156): "Past performance is no guarantee of future results." But that doesn't mean the past should be ignored, or worse, forgotten—especially when looking at the bigger picture. When it comes to understanding financial planning and investing, having a firm grasp on the history of the markets provides critical foundational knowledge.

These cycles of boom and bust discussed in the previous chapter have recurred time and again. And more broadly, when not booming or busting, the markets are usually traveling less dramatically up over time, and then down (or correcting) over time. Cycles, extreme or not, have occurred throughout history.

"It's déjà vu all over again."

—YOGI BERRA

So, if cycles repeat, why don't we simply follow the pattern to buy at the bottom and sell at the top? Cycles mimic the past in general terms (e.g., what goes up usually comes down and vice versa), but timing and duration don't have identical historical timelines. Industries, companies, information flow, political climate, investor sentiment, etc., constantly change and shift. That's why pinpointing the beginning or end of a particular cycle does not subject itself to formulaic analysis.

As an investor, understanding the history of financial markets and the relative position within a cycle (e.g., early- or late-stage; over- or undervalued) can help you assess risk and evaluate investment opportunities, but as far as pinpointing the exact optimal time to execute a trade, not so much. Refer to Chapter Ten and use your assessment of the cycle as another factor in evaluating the probability of specific investment alternatives and positioning yourself for the best *chance* at a positive outcome.

NOTE: If you would like more than just a few paragraphs on market cycles, I'd strongly suggest you read *Mastering the Market Cycle: Getting the Odds on Your Side* by Howard Marks. It's an in-depth and invaluable look at how investors should view and evaluate cycles to better position their portfolios.

Whether market returns have been strong to date (higher than long-term averages) or weak to date (lower than long-term averages) will help us assess where in the cycle we sit. And from this vantage point (the current relative level of returns) we can start to make an informed assessment of where returns are likely headed, even if we can't say exactly when.

Unless current market returns are approximately equal to the long-term historical average, you should not expect to receive the long-term historical average going forward. As the current market's yield moves away (up or down) from the long-term average, your expectations about future returns should move as well, in the opposite direction!

For 25 years, JP Morgan has been producing its annual Long-Term Capital Market Assumptions (LTCMA), providing their assessment of 10–15-year return projections for various asset classes.[69]

History teaches us, and JP Morgan reiterates, this fundamental truth: prices and future returns are inversely related. As the price of stocks rises, future returns will likely be lower. And the converse is true: as prices fall, future returns will likely rise.

Your life expectancy and withdrawal timeline play an enormous role in the outcome of your FI plan. If you have decades before reaching your FI date, using long-term market average returns might be a reasonable planning assumption for now. If you are close to your FI date (say within five to seven years), the long-term averages are less relevant, and you should focus on variable rates based on current valuation levels.

In late 2021, we are at all-time highs in the stock market. With high valuations, chances of a recession significantly increase, which will likely result in a period of below-average returns (including loss years). Reversion to the mean pulls averages toward their long-term trend line.

Those of us close to or actually withdrawing from our FI Portfolio should be focused on income and capital preservation. In such a scenario, your FI plan should manage the real risk of a drop in near-term equity returns. For example, consider holding more cash/bonds. Rebalance within equities to focus on dividend payers vs. pure growth investments. Interest, dividends, rents from real estate, etc. all serve to cushion the blow of market value declines. Investing in growth stocks with high valuations combined with a short time frame is the opposite of conservative. (We will discuss this concept in more detail in Chapter Fourteen.)

The long-term average market return (S&P 500 Index) is approximately 10% (1957–2020). This average is a simplistic summation of the long term, but it doesn't tell us much about the here and now. This reminds me of some statistician humor: There is a rather tall gentleman who lives in a rather small house. When he lies down, his head is in the oven and his feet are in the freezer. When asked how he felt, he responded, "On average, I feel fine."

Annual market returns are anything but average. How often does this S&P 500 Index average return actually occur within the "I feel fine" range of say 8–12%? In the 64 years since 1957, the annual return has been in the 8–12% range exactly five times. That's it. And the actual range of returns has been negative 37% (2008) to positive 43% (1958)—a spread of 80 percentage points!

> **NOTE:** Don't confuse "average" return with "expected" return. The stock market's long-term average return might be defined in the often-quoted tight range of 8-10%, but as the 80-percentage-point spread demonstrates, any given year's expected return can and likely will be different from the average, dramatically so in some years.

SMART MONEY IS SIMPLY DUMB MONEY THAT'S BEEN AROUND THE BLOCK A FEW TIMES

Following the 1932 bottom, the market return for the next 20 years averaged 15.4% per year. For the 20 years following the 1974 bottom, 15.1% per year. And for the 11 years following the March 2009 financial crisis bottom, 16% per year. Investing near the bottom of a market has proved time and again to be a profitable long-term strategy, but it takes a strong stomach to jump in and stay in when it seems that everyone else is running away.

What to do? If you're an investor in individual stocks, do your homework and focus on company fundamentals. If you're a passive index investor, keep investing. Yes, indexes come down too, but index funds don't file for bankruptcy and lose 100% of an investor's capital even if an individual company contained in the index does disappear.

> *"The trouble with most people is that they think with their hopes or fears or wishes rather than with their minds."*
>
> **—WILL DURANT**

As an example, if you had invested in a broad-based fund (S&P 500 Index fund) in March 2000, at the peak of the internet bubble, and held on through the crash without selling, five years later your portfolio would have been back to even. And if you used compounding portfolio growth during those five years and continued your dollar-cost averaging every month buying into that Index fund, your FI Portfolio balance would have been up by the time the market price got back to even!

Indexes eventually recover from their lows. That is the beauty of diversification. The stock that you directly own of a bankrupt liquidated company does not rise from the ashes—the loss is 100% permanent.

As individual investors, we can learn from historical markets and our own investing experiences. Keep your head out of the sand and pay attention.

Our goal with better understanding the past is not to predict the future but to see the present with clear eyes. To understand on a relative basis where the markets—and its participants—are today so we may better position our portfolio (aggressively or defensively). It is about relative decisions, not absolutes.

It's not about trying to time the exact top or bottom of a market. It is about situational awareness. For long-term investors, it's evaluating where we are in the current economic cycle so we can better assess what is *likely* to follow (but by no means guaranteed to follow). Don't go on your merry way investing with your eyes wide shut.

For example, if in your estimation the markets are closer to over-valued than undervalued, maybe consider keeping a little extra dry powder (i.e., cash) on hand to take advantage of tactical opportunities, opportunistic investing, but not wholesale strategic changes. Remember, our goal is meeting our future FI spending needs, not timing or beating the market.

It's not our planned actions that usually get investors in trouble, but rather our unplanned reactions to market events (e.g., selling after a crash or chasing overvalued stocks ever higher). Practice situational awareness. We can't possibly predict every bear market cycle or market crash, but we can better prepare psychologically for when dramatic market fluctuations inevitably arrive.

If investment managers wanted to better prepare investors, they could accurately amplify the generic disclaimer from the beginning of this chapter to say, "Past performance is no guarantee of future results because there is just too much luck involved in investing."

Researchers from Wake Forest University and Arizona State University tested the current disclaimer in an assessment of the effectiveness of mutual fund performance advertising. The study concluded that the disclaimer is "completely ineffective," and suggests that it should be expanded to include: "Studies show that mutual funds that have outperformed their peers in the past generally do not outperform them in the future. Strong past performance is often a matter of chance."[70] This suggestion for an expanded disclaimer, however, would not likely be viewed as a plus...at least not from the perspective of an investment manager's sales pitch.

"So we beat on, boats against the current, borne back ceaselessly into the past."

—F. SCOTT FITZGERALD

In 1997, Barry P. Barbash of the US Securities and Exchange Commission delivered a speech at the ICI Securities Law Procedures Conference in Washington, DC. The thrust of his speech was on some challenges facing the mutual fund industry at that time. He briefly reviewed the history of mutual funds as they gained in popularity during the 1960s only to fall out of favor in the 1970s. In summarizing his thoughts, Barbash observed, "We must remember the past because it has so much to teach us...We have an opportunity to learn from history and, in doing so, to avoid the pitfalls of the past. I can only hope we take full advantage of the opportunity." Channeling the philosopher George Santayana, Barbash concluded, "Some of us would prefer not to remember the past... But perhaps the only thing worse than remembering the past would be to relive it."[71]

As we discussed in earlier chapters, we need to use all the information we have at our disposal to make better-informed, probability-based decisions while always weighing the cost and consequences of being wrong.

Successful planning and investing are as much about being positioned for things to go right as they are being prepared for when things go wrong.

There are two types of investors in this world:

- Those who can extrapolate from incomplete data,

SUGGESTIONS FOR ADDITIONAL READING

Howard Marks, *Mastering the Market Cycle: Getting the Odds on Your Side* (Houghton Mifflin Harcourt, 2018).

13

MORE IS NEVER ENOUGH

"Life is a balance of holding on and letting go."

—RUMI

IN CHAPTER TWO, WE WORKED ON CALCULATING THE DOLLARS YOU need to meet your FI goals. But financial independence is about a lot more than just the math. While the numbers are extremely important, it's just as critical to answer the question: am I *comfortable* I have enough money? In addition to getting the math to work, you need to teach yourself to get comfortable and find inner peace with "enough" on an emotional and social level as well. This is true financial freedom.

I recently read an interview with Abigail Disney (granddaughter of Roy O. Disney, co-founder of the Walt Disney Company).[72] In it, they reference a study performed by *The Chronicle of Philanthropy* that asked people who inherited money a simple question: "What amount of money would you need to feel totally secure?" Regardless of the amount of money each had and inherited, every single person came up with an amount that was roughly twice what they inherited.

Money might not buy happiness but people expect, at a minimum, for money to get them far down the road. So how do you answer the question, "How much money is enough?" Early in the accumulation stage, the answer is likely self-evident: "More than I have today."

"More" is a lesson that we learn early on. More starts from early childhood and is one of the first math concepts understood by young children. And from a linguistics standpoint, it sure felt like my kids learned to say "more" right on the heels of learning "No!" ("Dad, can I borrow your car?" follows all too soon thereafter.)

Arguably, the desire for "more" is innate, but it is unquestionably clear that we as a society have stoked the fires of consumption. As we talked about previously, history can be instructive.

During the 1920s working hours were around 49 hours per week, then fell below 40 during the Great Depression. During World War II weekly hours again increased, but after World War II weekly working hours stabilized at 40.[73]

Early in the 20th century, the benefits of the Second Industrial Revolution had begun to curtail the need for a seemingly endless workweek and provided workers much-needed leisure time. As a result, there was considerable discussion and debate around the right balance of labor and leisure.[74]

Up until that time, individuals worked and made purchases to satisfy their basic needs. Once those needs were met, these same people could spend less time working and enjoy their new-found leisure. Businesses, however, began to worry about slowing economic growth and a national state of overproduction and saturation.

In response to the perceived threats of chronic overproduction and the declining need to work, business leaders began to refocus not on production but on consumption. They concluded that consumption (i.e., demand) could be stimulated and nurtured— with a little help from the advertising industry.

The Madison Avenue ad agencies (think the *Mad Men* TV show), in effect, helped usher in the concept of raising one's standard of living by buying not only what you *need*, but also what you *want*. And rather than individuals deciding on their own what they might want, businesses and advertisers would show them the way.

In 1929, President Herbert Hoover's Committee on Recent Economic Changes issued a report noting the following:

> The Survey has proved conclusively what has long been held theoretically to be true, that wants are almost insatiable; that one want satisfied makes way for another. The conclusion is that economically we have a boundless field before us; that there are new wants which will make way endlessly for newer wants, as fast as they are satisfied.[75]

Leisure time came to be seen not as a threat to working but as a compelling reason to work. People would need to work more to pay for the additional consumption of things they didn't previously know they wanted. And not expanding the 40-hour workweek was good because "it promises more leisure to use up golf balls and holiday clothes."[76]

The age of consumerism and the accumulation of things was upon us.

> **NOTE:** In 1939, Franklin D. Roosevelt upended a 150-year-old tradition by issuing a presidential proclamation moving up the Thanksgiving holiday by one week for the sole purpose of allowing more time for the Christmas shopping season. As a result of the proclamation, 32 states issued similar proclamations while 16 states refused to accept the change and proclaimed Thanksgiving to be the last Thursday in November. In 1941, after two years of national confusion, Congress established the fourth Thursday of November as the legal holiday.[77]

AN INTERESTING PARADOX

All this consumption is good for the macroeconomy: people spending money on goods and services. After all, personal consumption drives 70% of the US gross domestic product (GDP). It's just not a particularly good strategy for you as an individual on your FI wealth accumulation journey. If you spend all your earnings, you are helping to drive the economy but not growing your wealth. What helps you is everyone *else* spending and driving the economy up while *you* save and invest in companies that benefit from that economic growth. It is an interesting paradox: personal vs. societal economics. I let one simple rule guide me through this paradox on my FI journey: spend a little, save a lot.

IS MONEY THE ROOT OF ALL EVIL?

We are currently living in a culture of more. People constantly looking for more time, house, cars, vacations, sex, travel, and yes, money. Not that having more is bad, harmful, or immoral, but you do need to recognize that the *desire* to have more can be insatiable. It can become a vicious feedback loop—have some, want even more.

The Bible is often quoted as saying that money is the root of all evil. But what the Bible actually says is that "the love of money is the root of all evil." (1 Timothy 6:10). Money is not an end, in and of itself, but a tool to be used on your FI journey. We don't covet money, per se, but rather the freedom that money can offer us.

When it comes to your FI Portfolio, if you are not comfortable with your money being enough, the default solution will always be to seek out more. So, when does it end? When you mathematically have, and are emotionally comfortable with, enough. At that point, you will have reached financial freedom, or as financial author Brian Portnoy likes to call it, "funded contentment."

When the famed author of the bestselling World War II novel *Catch-22*, Joseph Heller, passed away, his contemporary and friend, Kurt Vonnegut, penned a short tribute. It recounted the tale of the two of them attending a party on Shelter Island, New

York, hosted by a billionaire hedge fund manager. Kurt informed Joe that their host likely made more money in one day than Joe's book had earned since it was published. Joe responded, "I've got something he can never have...enough."[78]

When the numbers add up and you have reached the promised land of financial independence, make sure your emotions and feelings about money are in the same place.

SUGGESTIONS FOR ADDITIONAL READING

Brian Portnoy, *The Geometry of Wealth: How to Shape a Life of Money and Meaning* (Harriman House, 2018).

John C. Bogle, *Enough: True Measures of Money, Business, and Life* (John Wiley & Sons, 2009).

14

THE FRAGILE DECADE

"Revenue is vanity, profit is sanity, but cash is king."

—UNKNOWN

ARE YOU FAMILIAR WITH THE FRAGILE DECADE? IT IS THE WONDER-fully exhilarating time that spans the last five years of working and the first five years of withdrawing from your FI Portfolio. It is also the period that could blow up your whole financial plan.

If you have not yet reached your fragile decade, pay even closer attention because this is a glimpse into your financial future—a future that you can be better prepared to take on when it arrives faster than you currently imagine.

Think about mountain climbing. The journey begins with careful planning for the ascent up the mountain to eventually attain the summit. But mountain climbing isn't only about standing on the peak, it's also about getting back down safely. Mountain climbers often say that planning and executing the descent is more involved and difficult than the journey up.

And just like mountain climbing, both stages of our financial plan, the ascent (accumulation) and descent (withdrawal), are best executed when planned out before ever stepping foot on the mountain.

Some investors are obsessively focused on the ascent—accumulating wealth, getting to the peak, and quitting their job. But having read the previous chapters, you know we must plan for not only getting *to* the withdrawal stage but also getting *through* it. As we discussed in Chapter One, the goal is for your FI Portfolio to provide you an acceptable monthly cash flow that you don't outlive—a comfortable, stress-free walk around and down the mountain.

ONCE YOU'VE WON THE GAME, STOP PLAYING!

Please notice that nowhere in this goal do we talk about beating the market. As you approach your fragile decade and put your focus on covering your monthly expenses, you should realize that success is best measured by meeting *your* goals, not beating some arbitrary market benchmark. Said another way, your primary objective during the withdrawal stage is not to maximize returns, but rather to meet your spending needs. Your goals not only help you to design your plan, but they are also the driving force and the endgame.

NOTE: At best, your rate of return is indicative of only a piece of your FI Portfolio performance. Remember, compounding portfolio growth requires both investment returns and monthly contributions to reach its full potential. Using your spending goals as your benchmark, you'll force yourself to appropriately consider both components of compounding portfolio growth in your periodic status assessments.

Now that you are close to or in the fragile decade, your clearly defined spending goals will dictate how conservative or aggressive your go-forward plan needs to be, how much cushion you have or want to add, and how simple or complex your plan should be. In measuring your success, your personal monthly spending need is your ultimate yardstick and the only benchmark that matters. At times, staying focused on your personal goals won't be easy. As John Pierpont Morgan once observed, "Nothing so undermines your financial judgment as the sight of your neighbor getting rich." So, hang tough and keep reminding yourself: to hell with "keeping up with the Joneses" or "beating the market." Take a deep breath and realize the only person you need to beat tomorrow is the person you are today. Meeting your personal goals is what matters.

"Money is in some respects like fire; it is a very excellent servant but a terrible master."

—PHINEAS TAYLOR BARNUM

When someone asks me how I'm doing with my investing, the question usually comes out something like this: *The market was up 12% last year; how'd you do?* I would sometimes respond with: "My portfolio grew (from both returns and contributions) at a rate consistent with my long-term plan to achieve my date-specific goal of financial independence, which will generate a monthly cash flow I won't outlive." You can imagine the twisted faces and quizzical looks that response generated. Not nearly as much fun as declaring triumphantly, "I almost beat the market!"

If an advisor says to you (or you tell yourself) that you beat the market last year, your response should be, *An interesting factoid, but not my primary focus.* Much more importantly, *Where am I relative to my FI plan goals, and do I need to course-correct?*

> **NOTE:** As discussed in Chapter Five, the rate of return can be a useful tool as you benchmark and evaluate the investment performance of an advisor. After all, investment returns are a component of your FI plan, just not a goal of your plan.

"The future is the worst thing about the present."
—GUSTAVE FLAUBERT

What about market risk? A prolonged downturn in the market during the fragile decade can derail withdrawal plans. The conventional approach to managing through market declines and loss years is to take the long view, keep investing, and rely on long-term averages to eventually help the portfolio recover. This approach can work well when you are younger, have salary income, and have decades to ride out the storm before taking withdrawals. For those of us near or in the fragile decade, the long view may not be the optimal course of action, or worse, it could be downright devastating. (We will walk through an example a little later.)

As you approach your FI date, you should have a much more accurately defined and refined list of FI spending needs. As a result, this is when your investment strategy for the withdrawal stage can (and likely will) diverge from the accumulation stage. A lot of the investing concepts we've discussed for the accumulation stage (and that are put forth by financial advisors) are grounded in modern portfolio theory (MPT), which seeks to optimize market returns and risk by asset class. Simply stated, as you invest for the long term, get as much of a return as you can, given your level of risk tolerance.

> **NOTE:** Harry Markowitz introduced the world to MPT in 1952 and his principles have influenced generations of financial thinking. In 1990, Markowitz shared the Nobel Prize in Economics for his efforts around MPT.

Finding this optimal balance of return and risk is what Markowitz describes as investing along the efficient frontier. MPT has been successfully used for decades by institutions such as endowments, pension plans, and large trust funds, etc. The traditional approach to retirement planning has taken the principles of MPT and adapted them to individual investors.

But here's the rub: large institutions, like an endowment, have an infinite time horizon without a fragile decade. Institutions are effectively in a perpetual accumulation stage. They do not need to plan for and manage through a significant and finite withdrawal stage, but you do.

> *"If you want something you've never had, you must be willing to do something you've never done."*
>
> —THOMAS JEFFERSON[79]

Enter: goals-based planning. With origins going back decades, goals-based planning gained in popularity after the 2008–2009 financial crisis. It seeks to refocus our goals away from obtaining abstract market return rates, and toward meeting specific personal goals (e.g., our monthly spending needs).

As such, we should similarly reframe our FI risk profile, moving away from focusing on the volatility of market prices. Technical definitions of market risk include such terms as standard deviation, alpha, beta, R-squared, and Sharpe ratio. But as we look at our FI plan, we can describe our risk in a simpler, more holistic way: **our principal risk is the chance that we fall short of our FI spending goals.**

I first happened upon this practical definition of risk years ago while reading Peter Bernstein's bestselling book, *Against the Gods: The Remarkable Story of Risk.* In the book, investment manager Robert Jeffrey explains that volatility is not a good measure of risk because on its own, it is simply a probability statistic. Volatility needs to be linked with a consequence to provide a practical measure of risk. For example, the fundamental risk in your FI Portfolio is not having the cash, when you need it, to make essential expenditures.[80]

I generally don't shy away from an investment because its price might be volatile, but I'll stay away if I think there is a relatively high probability that I'll permanently lose my money. Always evaluate the probability of a good investment outcome against the consequences of being wrong.

> **NOTE:** In this context, if our goal is to accumulate wealth over the long term (decades), then a balanced stock fund is arguably less risky than bonds. Stock prices are generally more volatile than bonds, but remember, our primary risk is not volatility, but rather missing our spending goals, and over the long term, stocks (as an asset class) generally return more than bonds. Even if you are retired, some portion of your portfolio might not be touched for 20-30 years, if ever. Again, if you are looking to grow this legacy portion of the portfolio, a balanced stock fund is likely to grow more than bonds. The key here is *"over the long term."* Money you need for short-term goals should not be in stocks.

A goals-based approach to planning can help make the risk more tangible. We take measured, personally defined risks, and don't endlessly ponder esoteric volatility measures of risk. Goals-based planning is focused on optimizing a limited pool of financial assets by matching assets and income with future liabilities and expenses (i.e., future spending needs).

If, for example, you can meet all your cash flow needs with a 5%
return, then why take on a greater risk of loss to try and achieve
a higher return? To paraphrase Warren Buffett, why risk losing
what you have and need to chase what you don't have and don't
need? Your goals, not your risk tolerance, should drive investing
decisions. During the withdrawal stage, income and capital preservation become more important than stretching for outsized
returns.

	Traditional Approach	Goals-Based Investing
Purpose	Matching or beating a benchmark index	Funding personal FI spending goals
Performance Evaluation	Compared to a benchmark	Progress toward goals
Definition of Risk	Volatility (standard deviation)	Coming up short of a goal
Aggressiveness in Portfolio	As much as you can endure (Risk Tolerance)	As little as you need (Risk Capacity)

IF YOU DON'T KNOW WHERE YOUR LAST DOLLAR WENT, IT'S TOUGHER TO PLAN WHERE YOUR NEXT DOLLAR WILL GO

Under the umbrella of goals-based planning, the idea of a safety-first
strategy has evolved. This concept has been around for a long time,
but has been brought to a wider audience more recently by several

folks, including Boston University professor Zvi Bodie and Rachelle Taqqu in their book *Risk Less and Prosper*, and through the work of Professor Wade Pfau of the America College of Financial Services and author of the book *Safety-First Retirement Planning*.

In a nutshell, a goals-based safety-first strategy looks at your FI spending goals in two broad baskets. The first, the safe basket, seeks to cover your basic financial *needs* (e.g., housing, food, healthcare, contingency fund, etc.) with assets invested with as little risk as possible (i.e., the safety-first component).

To start, you might think of safety-first investments such as bank CDs, money-market funds, short-duration government bonds, and bond ladders, etc. But don't lose sight of other financial resources you might have beyond cash and bonds that could also provide safety-first withdrawals—for example, Social Security, a pension, rental income from real estate, income annuities, and insurance products. The key is to build a stream of income that will cover your basic needs regardless of a declining stock market.

Dividends from long-term holdings (for example, an S&P 500 Index fund) **might** be appropriate to add to the income from your more traditional "safety-first" investments—**but only if** you are holding high-quality, dividend-paying investments for the long term. In this scenario, the price volatility of the underlying stocks becomes less relevant because you don't have a plan, or a need, to sell the investment—somewhat analogous to a real estate investor collecting rents from their apartment building. The monthly rental income is what matters. Daily changes in the market value of the building are of no consequence to the long-term investor. By no means are dividends guaranteed, but historically, dividends have been less volatile than stock prices.

NOTE: Since 1950, there have been 10 bear markets defined by a 20% or greater drop in the S&P 500 Index (excluding the COVID-19-induced drop which has yet to completely play out). In half of them, dividends increased. In four of the remaining five, the average peak-to-trough decline in dividends was just 4%. The average number of years it took for dividends to get back to their previous high was 2.5 years. The one outlier is the 2008–2009 financial crisis, which saw the S&P 500 Index drop 57%. The dividend decline was 24%, less than half of the Index drop. It took four years for the dividends to recover to their precrisis level.[81]

If a decrease in dividends would cause you to miss your basic needs goal, consider counting something less than 100% of your dividend income in your "safety-first" basket. For example, maybe you only count two-thirds of your dividends (effectively reserving one-third) and put one-third into the second basket for discretionary spending.

Once this safety-first basket is secure, you can then put the remainder of your portfolio in the second, or aggressive, basket to cover discretionary spending (*wants*); this basket can be invested as aggressively (or conservatively) as you see fit. When your basic needs are met, you can decide how much risk you want to take to achieve your aspirational wants—those items that would be "nice to have" (more frequent vacations, etc.), but in a falling stock market, you could do without.

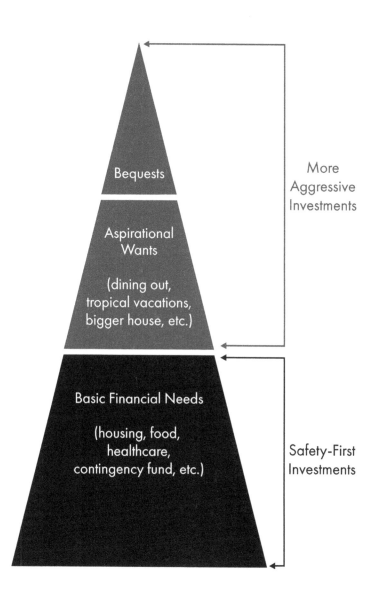

"Markets can remain irrational longer than you and I can remain solvent."

—A. GARY SHILLING[82]

One of the most significant reasons that the fragile decade can be so perilous is the effects of sequence risk. This is the danger that the order (i.e., sequence) of market returns will have a material negative impact on your planned withdrawals. Let's look at a simple example to explain the math. Assume you retired at age 57 with $1 million at the beginning of 2000. You started with an annual withdrawal of 4% of your portfolio ($40,000), which you increased each year by 3% for inflation. Sequence 1, in the below chart, shows that by 2020, at 77 years young, you would have enough to cover just two more years of withdrawals (and this assumes you had no unexpected expenses over the 20 years).

Sequence 2 has identical assumptions, except that the sequence of the returns is different (I simply reversed the order of the returns). You can see that in both sequences you achieved the same average annual return (7% simple average) and total withdrawals ($1.1 million). In Sequence 2, however, you would have reached age 77 with almost $1.8 million *remaining* in your FI Portfolio—$776,000 *more* than you retired with. The sequence of returns matters!

> **NOTE:** For those of you who think the hypothetical returns in the above example look far-fetched, Sequence 1 lists the actual annual returns of the S&P 500 Index (including dividends) in chronological order.[83]

Year	Age	Sequence 1			Sequence 2		
		Hypothetical Returns	Annual Withdrawal	FI Portfolio Balance $1,000,000	Hypothetical Returns - REVERSED	Annual Withdrawal	FI Portfolio Balance $1,000,000
2000	57	-9.10%	40,000	872,640	18.40%	40,000	1,262,304
2001	58	-11.89%	41,200	732,582	31.49%	41,200	1,167,620
2002	59	-22.10%	42,436	537,624	-4.38%	42,436	1,370,811
2003	60	28.68%	43,709	635,569	21.83%	43,709	1,485,824
2004	61	10.88%	45,020	654,801	11.96%	45,020	1,460,686
2005	62	4.91%	46,371	638,303	1.38%	46,371	1,607,935
2006	63	15.79%	47,762	683,788	13.69%	47,762	2,065,513
2007	64	5.49%	49,195	669,432	32.39%	49,195	2,338,929
2008	65	-37.00%	50,671	389,820	16.00%	50,671	2,336,540
2009	66	26.46%	52,191	426,965	2.11%	52,191	2,628,373
2010	67	15.06%	53,757	429,414	15.06%	53,757	3,255,859
2011	68	2.11%	55,369	381,937	26.46%	55,369	2,016,309
2012	69	16.00%	57,030	376,891	-37.00%	57,030	2,066,843
2013	70	32.39%	58,741	421,199	5.49%	58,741	2,325,180
2014	71	13.69%	60,504	410,074	15.79%	60,504	2,375,872
2015	72	1.38%	62,319	352,555	4.91%	62,319	2,565,268
2016	73	11.96%	64,188	322,855	10.88%	64,188	3,218,390
2017	74	21.83%	66,114	312,788	28.68%	66,114	2,455,623
2018	75	-4.38%	68,097	233,973	-22.10%	68,097	2,103,649
2019	76	31.49%	70,140	215,424	-11.89%	70,140	1,848,459
2020	77	18.40%	72,244	$169,524	-9.10%	72,244	$1,776,215
Avg. Annual Return		7%			7%		
Total Withdrawals			$1,147,059			$1,147,059	

Source for S&P 500 returns: https://www.slickcharts/sp500/returns

The above period, 2000–2020, illustrates the negative impact on withdrawals of down markets, especially early on. But to be fair, there are plenty of other periods where the results would not be disastrous and in fact could *grow* the portfolio, or allow you to withdraw more, like Sequence 2. That's why it's a risk—you just don't know what kind of sequence you're going to be dealt as you enter the withdrawal stage. Luck of the draw.

The premise of our goals-based safety-first strategy is to rely as little as possible on the sale of stocks to cover basic needs in the short term due to the price volatility. As Sequence 1 shows us, there is nothing safe about needing to sell stocks to meet FI spending goals when the market is falling.

So how do we minimize sequence risk during the withdrawal stage? Consider two action steps.

- First, **add a margin of safety to your projections**. Lower your projected withdrawal rate in your modeling to account for the sequence of return risk (that is, the risk that you start withdrawing during a bad stretch of market returns). Financial author William Bernstein calculated that a particularly bad sequence of returns can penalize your safe withdrawal amount by about 1.5%–2%.[84] So, for example, if you are projecting a 5% withdrawal rate, consider lowering that estimate to an amount closer to 3%–3.5% to provide cushion against "bad" market returns in the early years of the withdrawal stage. This may also lead you to conclude that you need to make other course corrections—for example, targeting a larger FI Portfolio balance on your FI date than you originally assumed. Simply put, plan to spend less and save more.

- Second, **maintain a cash reserve**. As you approach your FI date, have a cash cushion. For example, keep three to five years (or more) of spending needs out of the stock market and in cash. Since you hopefully won't need to sell and withdraw from the equity portion of the portfolio if the market is declining, you avoid the negative compounding effects we saw illustrated in Sequence 1 of the example. (Remember, compounding works with you during the accumulation stage and against you in the withdrawal stage.) And as the market eventually recovers, you can then sell some of your equity investments to replenish your cash reserve. Three to five years of cash is my personal comfort zone. What do others say?

Author and investor Darrow Kirkpatrick found that the S&P 500 recovers from declines, *on average*, in about three years. For business cycle declines going back to the 1800s, it's about five years. Citing research by Wade Pfau, Kirkpatrick notes that worst-case real stock market losses of greater than 50% take, on average, nine years to recover.[85]

Based on Kirkpatrick's findings, on a worst-case basis, you might consider having upwards of 10 years of spending needs in cash, plus potentially more in other conservative investments.[86]

> **NOTE:** The more you hold in cash and the longer you hold it, the higher the probability that your FI Portfolio's overall rate of return will diminish. Cash provides safety to cover expenses when stocks are declining, but that safety comes at the cost of virtually no investment return on that cash, especially in this ultra-low-interest-rate environment. Recognize this trade-off and be sure to factor it into your overall plan.

The above suggestions are but two considerations as you make personal course corrections to your robust financial plan. My primary message is this: make sure to reconcile cash withdrawal plans with what your modeling and current market conditions indicate you can support. In other words, as you approach the withdrawal stage, don't take as much risk as you can tolerate; take as little risk as you need.

With a focus on safety first to cover basic spending needs and the right balance of liquidity, the fragile decade can be a lot less frail.

A FEW MORE THOUGHTS ON RISK TOLERANCE

The traditional approach to assessing your risk tolerance would have you complete a questionnaire about your investing experience and your rational response to some hypothetical questions. Tally up your score and you find yourself plotted along a continuum that might look something like this five-point scale: conservative, moderately conservative, moderate, moderately aggressive, aggressive.

The problem is, you may answer the questions on some random Saturday afternoon when the sun is shining and the stock market is closed. Now answer the questions when the stock market has been falling for five straight days and the talk of recession is flashing all over the financial news...do you think you might vacillate over these same questions?

Calculating "risk tolerance" based on volatility is an interesting theoretical analysis, but when mixed with emotions, it can provide an investor with a misleading and sometimes erroneous answer.

In a 2020 study, researchers in the UK found that emotions toward investments are quite important in explaining the variations in financial risk tolerance among investors. The study found that emotions exceed the impact of traditional inputs to a risk tolerance assessment such as gender, age, income, investment experience, and knowledge.[87]

The study also points out that attitudes toward risk are not static and suggests that more research should be done to reassess the extent to which risk tolerance varies over time for a given individual.

Their study brought the authors to this conclusion: "It is clear that omitting emotional factors from theoretical or empirical models is likely to result in a very incomplete view of how people make financial decisions."[88]

"Volatility is the emotional cost of the growth we seek."

—BRIAN PORTNOY

Theoretical risk analysis will drift when emotions are factored in. Even the father of modern portfolio theory, Harry Markowitz, couldn't initially overcome the emotional roller coaster. Shortly after publishing his groundbreaking article on MPT, he was asked how he allocated his portfolio. Rather than following his own efficient frontier guidance, Markowitz ignored his own research as his emotionally charged risk analysis interceded.

Attempting to minimize future regret, he simply split his contributions equally between bonds and equities. Later, Markowitz reevaluated his allocations and made course corrections to his portfolio, but only after defeating or at least reaching a draw with his emotions.[89]

Focus on your goals, not volatility, to keep you from floundering about in a sea of emotional uncertainty.

SUGGESTIONS FOR ADDITIONAL READING

Zvi Bodie and Rachelle Taqqu, *Risk Less and Prosper: Your Guide to Safer Investing* (John Wiley & Sons, 2012).

Wade Pfau, *Safety-First Retirement Planning: An Integrated Approach for a Worry-Free Retirement* (Retirement Researcher Media, 2019).

Robert C. Carlson, *The New Rules of Retirement: Strategies for a Secure Future* (John Wiley & Sons, 2016).

Howard Marks, *The Most Important Thing Illuminated: Uncommon Sense for the Thoughtful Investor* (in particular, the discussion of "risk" in Chapters 5–7) (Columbia University Press, 2013).

Steven Bavaria, *The Income Factory: An Investor's Guide to Consistent Lifetime Returns* (McGraw Hill Education, 2020).

15

"SAFE" WITHDRAWAL RATE AND THE 4% RULE

"Knowing is not enough; we must apply. Willing is not enough; we must do."

—JOHANN WOLFGANG VON GOETHE

WHEN PLANNING FOR THE WITHDRAWAL STAGE, SEVERAL VARIABLES impact your plan: rate of return, number of years in the plan, asset allocation, sequence of returns, etc. As we saw in the previous chapter, some of these variables are out of your control (e.g., sequence of returns). The single largest variable, however, is likely the dollar amount of your annual withdrawals (just as contributions are critical during the accumulation stage), and this variable is completely within your control.

One of the earliest published strategies for withdrawing from your FI Portfolio has come to be known as the safe spending rate, or simply, the 4% Rule. In short, you withdraw 4% of your FI Portfolio in your initial year. In subsequent years, you increase the dollar amount of your withdrawal to account for inflation. In theory, by following this strategy, you should have a high probability of your annual withdrawals lasting 30 years.

For example, let's say you have $1 million in your FI Portfolio at the beginning of your withdrawal stage. In year one, you could withdraw $40,000. If inflation (i.e., the cost of living) rises 3% that year, then in year two, you withdraw $41,200 ($40,000 plus 3%), and so on for 30 years.

Seems like a simple enough shortcut to follow, but first, recognize it as such—a shortcut. As we discussed in Chapter Nine, when blindly accepted as golden rules, shortcuts can be dangerous to your financial and emotional well-being.

"Try and fail, but don't fail to try."

—JOHN QUINCY ADAMS

Let's start with a holistic view of withdrawal strategies. My experience shows that there are four levels in the progression of thinking about "your FI number" and withdrawals from your portfolio:

Level One: Financial novices throw out numbers off the top of their heads without any real data to back them up. I've heard guesses at the presumed FI number in the range of $500,000 to $25 million. That's a big range! And that range tells us nothing about how much a person could annually withdraw. Fun to banter around with friends, but not a lot of practical guidance at this level.

Level Two: Some advisors suggest that you use your pre-FI *income* to estimate your targeted FI spending needs. That is, multiply your salary by some factor (often 70%–85%) to estimate what you will need in annual FI cash flow. This implies that your spending is directly tied to your historical level of income. If you are living paycheck to paycheck, this estimate may be somewhat reliable. For diligent FI enthusiasts who annually save increasing amounts of their income, this method could significantly overstate FI cash flow needs.

Level Three: You gain more focus and clarity by estimating spending needs based on your projected future *expenses* rather than a percentage of historical income. You then take your annual cash flow need and multiply it by 25 to get to your targeted FI number (this is effectively getting at the 4% Rule).

Level Four: FI enthusiasts and advisors work past these "rules of thumb" and averages, and focus on projecting a *personalized* withdrawal dollar amount based on your spending needs (resulting in a personal withdrawal rate that could be higher or lower than the shortcut *average* 4% rate).

You cannot get to 100% certainty of never running out of money (remember, no one can predict the future with complete accuracy), but these four levels coincide with increasing confidence levels. If you are the freewheeling, fly-by-the-seat-of-your-pants type, pick a number at Level One, and never worry about it again! Since you are reading this book, I would suggest you are already past Level One and looking to refine your number and gain more confidence in your personal withdrawal strategy.

The concept that has become known as the "4% Rule" was first introduced by financial advisor Bill Bengen in 1994. I often hear it referenced as the goalpost for withdrawal planning purposes. But Mr. Bengen has been clear in pointing out that his research is based on a worst-case scenario using a very specific set of assumptions, including a targeted asset allocation of 50% stocks and 50% intermediate-term US government bonds, historical market results, and a fixed 30-year retirement period.

Your personal savings rate, spending, and withdrawal needs; your asset allocation; your time horizon; your actual market returns, etc. will all impact what withdrawal rate(s) will work (and not work) for you. If you're early in your wealth accumulation stage with decades to go, being familiar with the 4% Rule can give you a big-picture view of the distant future. That is, for each $1 million in your FI Portfolio, you may be able to generate roughly $40,000 of annual cash flow. It's a helpful shortcut but only for a very high-level estimation.

> **NOTE:** The 4% Rule from different angles. The Annual Rule of 25: every $1 in *annual* expense will require $25 in your FI Portfolio so, to cover a $1,000 recurring annual expense you would need $25,000 in your FI Portfolio ($1,000 × 25). The Monthly Rule of 300: for every $1 of *monthly* expense, you will need $300 in your FI Portfolio. For example, to cover a $500 monthly expense, you need $150,000 in your portfolio ($500 × 300).

The 4% Rule has been back-tested and is a great starting point, but do not use it as an endpoint unless you have run the numbers based on your circumstances. Your personal situation might indicate a higher or lower initial withdrawal rate. Go back and look at the example in Chapter Fourteen. Scenario 1 showed us that blindly following an initial 4% withdrawal rate would not have worked for that year-2000 retiree with an S&P 500 portfolio. And in Scenario 2, a higher than 4% withdrawal rate could have been supported. Let the 4% Rule inform your plan, not be your plan.

Since Bill Bengen's groundbreaking work, many investment advisors have done their own analysis and offer advice on "safe" withdrawal rates that are, not surprisingly, similar to Bengen's. For example, Fidelity offers up a rule of thumb of starting with no more than a 4% to 5% initial withdrawal rate and caveats that personal circumstances could impact that rate. Fidelity's website also has a free calculator that gives you some high-level projections of what your initial withdrawal rate might be (again with all the appropriate caveats).[90]

AS THE WINDS OF CHANGE BLOW, PUT UP A SAIL, NOT A WALL

The point is, no amount of historical research and back-testing can give you an absolute withdrawal rate going forward. Rather than a rule or *goalpost*, use 4% as a *guidepost* in your financial planning and annual updates. Adjust for your personal circumstances accordingly.

This 4% guidepost can help calibrate your withdrawal planning. Let's say you are still in the accumulation stage and are dutifully projecting out through your withdrawal stage (as discussed in

Chapter Two). If your projected withdrawal rate is less than 4%, Bengen's historical research will likely give you a relatively high level of comfort that your plan could be achievable. If, however, you find that a 4% withdrawal won't get you the dollars you want, or your cash withdrawals won't last for as many years as you want, then you may need to course-correct (increase contributions, reduce spending goals, work longer, revisit withdrawal strategies, etc.).

> **NOTE:** One course correction I would not make is trying to outperform the market to increase your investment return. While a higher than market rate of return would mathematically increase your cash withdrawals, this is a highly unlikely outcome for most investors, including professionals. See Chapters Five and Six for a refresher on why this is so. A better course correction would be to increase your savings rate (contributions) during the accumulation stage.

Below is a chart of the maximum sustainable withdrawal rates (based on Bengen's research) prepared by Wade Pfau in 2018. As you can see, the so-called SAFEMAX (a term Bengen used to describe the highest sustainable withdrawal rate for the worst-case scenario in the time period covered) is approximately 4%.

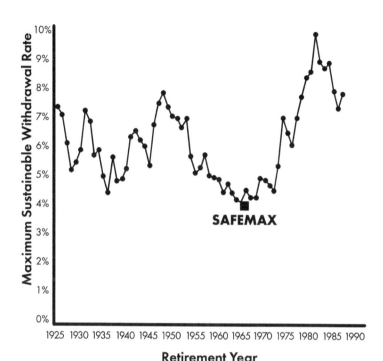

Maximum Sustainable Withdrawal Rates For 50/50 Asset Allocation, 30-Year Retirement, Inflation Adjustments Using SBBI Data, 1926-2017, S&P 500 and Intermediate-Term Government Bonds

Source: Forbes[91]

But look at the variability of results depending on the year of retirement. The range is approximately 4% for a retiree in 1966 to over 9% for a retiree in 1982.

Rather than thinking of 4% as the target, think of it as being on the lower end of a range—a range of possible outcomes. With the use of probabilities, you can then calibrate your projections knowing that moving toward 4% (or below) is conservative and moving above 4% is potentially aggressive but not out of the question.

Does that mean I would recommend planning for the high end of the range? Absolutely not. While 9% would have worked in one 30-year period, it would have failed in all the rest! I also wouldn't be banking on 4% as a sure thing (the past does not predict the future). This is why you need to run multiple projected scenarios with a range of possible withdrawal rates and course-correct based on personal circumstances.

WANNA BET? (REMEMBER CHAPTER TEN)

When you think in ranges and consider the probability of a certain outcome, you will develop a range of possible outcomes that you have a reasonable chance of achieving. And a small range of reasonable possibilities will serve you better than one answer that is precisely calculated but improbable. Improbable because with so many variables, and an unknown future, precision is an illusion.

Twenty-five years after first publishing his findings, Bill Bengen discussed the oversimplified interpretation of the 4% Rule that has found a wide audience. Bengen noted that 4% is based on empirical research but it's not (and never has been) an unassailable truth. There is no one-size-fits-all and your personal withdrawal rate could be any amount.[92]

In effect, the withdrawal stage is the mirror image of the accumulation stage. Just as your level of contributions has a significant impact on accumulating wealth, annual withdrawals have a significant *negative* compounding impact on your FI Portfolio. Compounding works with you during the accumulation stage and against you during the withdrawal stage. Tread lightly in planning out your withdrawal stage (especially in the early years), and annually reassess, course-correcting when necessary.

> **NOTE:** Which would make you feel better: (1) planning for a 3-4% withdrawal range and later realizing you can take larger withdrawals, or (2) counting on a 6-7% withdrawal range and later realizing you must cut back and live on less?

While this chapter has focused on one aspect of withdrawal planning (the withdrawal rate), it also highlights the importance of always stepping back and looking at the bigger picture—having a holistic view. Asset allocation, number of years, risk appetite, sequence of returns, etc. will all have an impact on your *personal* "safe" withdrawal rate.

Four percent might work for the average person, but as we've discussed elsewhere, no one individual is the "average person." Everyone is unique, and while 4% might work in a hypothetical example with one set of specific variables, change one or more of those variables and all bets are off. You need to assess *your* Life's Complete Financial Arc.

The key is to not have a rigid withdrawal plan, but a flexible and personalized strategy—for example, developing a plan that contemplates variable annual withdrawals providing flexibility to take less when market valuations are down (e.g., temporarily lowering your vacation spending or dining out expenses), and to take more when valuations are higher. Being flexible can increase the likelihood that your money will last as long as you do.

PCR: Plan, Course-Correct, Repeat.

SUGGESTIONS FOR ADDITIONAL READING

Zvi Bodie and Rachelle Taqqu, *Risk Less and Prosper: Your Guide to Safer Investing* (John Wiley & Sons, 2012).

Wade Pfau, *How Much Can I Spend in Retirement?: A Guide to Investment-Based Retirement Income Strategies* (Retirement Researcher Media, 2017).

Robert C. Carlson, *The New Rules of Retirement: Strategies for a Secure Future* (John Wiley & Sons, 2016).

16

THE RISING GENERATION

"Don't judge each day by the harvest you reap but by the seeds that you plant."

—ROBERT LOUIS STEVENSON

HOW MUCH MONEY SHOULD YOU LEAVE YOUR CHILDREN? AS MUCH AS THEY ARE PROPERLY PREPARED TO MANAGE

ACCORDING TO ONE ESTIMATE, SOME 45 MILLION US HOUSEHOLDS will transfer over $68 trillion in wealth over the next 25 years. Seventy percent of that wealth ($48 trillion) will come from baby boomers.[93] This great wealth transfer won't happen all at once, but it will happen. There is, however, the question of where the wealth will go.

Unlike prior generations, who most likely would leave wealth to heirs, baby boomers are a somewhat different breed. Compared to their predecessors, boomers are likely to live longer, spend more, and give more to charity.

Let's look at this wealth transfer from two different perspectives: first from the wealth creator's point of view, and second from the potential heir's point of view.

PART ONE: TRANSFERRING WEALTH TO THE RISING (NEXT) GENERATION

If you choose to leave some amount of wealth to heirs, the questions center around how and when to transfer your wealth. The most common strategy (if for no other reason than it requires very little forethought) is to keep all your wealth until you die and simply bequeath it to your designated heirs upon your departure from this earth.

There is a simple elegance in passing on wealth in this manner, but it also comes with one potentially significant foot fault. Will your heirs know what to do with the inheritance?

I'm sure they will know how to spend some cash on items they heretofore hadn't purchased. (Anecdotally, I once read that it takes the average heir just 19 days before they buy a new car.) This may all be well and good, but what if you leave a more significant sum of money?

If you do choose to leave significant wealth to the rising generation, here are some sobering observations for you to ponder: 70% of wealthy families will lose their wealth by the second generation and 90% will lose it by the third generation.[94] This means that in only 3 out of 10 families will grandchildren receive anything from the original wealth creator, and in 9 out of 10 families, great-grandchildren will get nothing!

Transferring wealth, therefore, is not simply about giving the next generation a pot of cash. It's about sharing with them your wisdom and equipping them with the tools necessary to live the productive life that financial independence can provide.

> *"Nothing fails like success because we don't learn from it. We learn only from failure."*
>
> **—KENNETH EWART BOULDING**

Why is it that so many wealth creators pass on their money to wealth spenders? It comes down to education and awareness. The rising generation, the children of the wealthy, often lack the financial education and entrepreneurial spirit to manage and grow wealth. They were not the ones who spent decades patiently accumulating wealth, dealing with the occasional mistakes and losses, all while following a well-thought-out, disciplined planning process. So, it shouldn't surprise you that some heirs have not developed the skills to manage and grow a substantial portfolio, especially when it shows up all at once on their doorstep as a lump-sum inheritance windfall!

There is a misguided belief among some future heirs that an inheritance equals immediate retirement and is a cure-all for financial ills—but you know better. Time and again, this belief proves to be nothing but false hope.

Remember back in Chapter Ten we discussed "Commodore" Cornelius Vanderbilt and the railroad empire he built? When adjusted for inflation, the Commodore left more than $100 billion to his heirs when he died in 1877. The Commodore left the bulk of his fortune to his son, William, who doubled it in the eight short years before his death at age 64. Then the train went off the rails. The first Vanderbilt family reunion was held in 1973. Of the 120 Vanderbilt descendants gathered at Vanderbilt University, not one was a millionaire.[95]

It goes to show how even the largest of fortunes can one day evaporate if not responsibly managed and occasionally replenished by future generations.

Responsibility for financial assets without *readiness* is a dangerous combination. This ineptitude with handling a large amount of money is similar to the sudden wealth syndrome experienced by some lottery winners and professional athletes. We have all heard stories of lottery winners squandering their money within a few short years. Professional athletes with big paydays and relatively short careers are not immune.

If you are not prepared, a sudden fortune can lead to feeling overwhelmed, overspending, and making poor decisions, all with potentially disastrous ramifications.

According to a 2018 story in *Sports Illustrated*, by the time professional NFL players have been retired for two years, 78% of them are bankrupt or under financial stress because of joblessness or divorce. An estimated 60% of former NBA players are broke within five years of retirement, and numerous retired MLB players have been similarly ruined.[96]

It's easy enough to bequest money through your last will and testament, but no will can pass on the financial savvy and the wealth creation mindset that you have nurtured over your lifetime. Without FI training and encouragement, your children might easily become just another tale of an inheritance squandered, giving further support to the grim statistics cited earlier. After a lifetime of growing your wealth, this is probably not the future you are hoping for or likely the one the Commodore envisioned.

> *"If you don't watch out, you can set up a situation where a child never has the pleasure of bringing home a paycheck."*
>
> **—T. BOONE PICKENS, JR.**

So, as the wealth creator, what are you to do? Well before you give money to your heirs, give them an even more important gift: the wisdom you have spent decades accumulating. Teach them to strive for financial independence (regardless of any potential inheritance). Encourage in them the entrepreneurial spirit to work hard, accumulate wealth, set their own financial goals, and chart their course to achieve those goals. To teach financial independence, it is a good idea to help them be independent in all aspects of their life.

Financial planner Jill Shipley eloquently explains:

> There is value in the struggle, lessons in failure, and character forged in the journey, so support and equip them but don't overprotect or control them. All the money in the world can't give your child (internal and external) credibility—they need to earn it themselves.[97]

Teach them that an inheritance might be a pleasant addition to their plan, but hoping for a windfall should not be *the* plan.

When educating potential heirs about inheritances, don't focus on the dollar amount they might receive, but rather the values and financial wisdom you've spent a lifetime shaping and accumulating. No matter what else you leave to your children, give them the two gifts that will bear fruit for generations to come: your unconditional love and the gift of wisdom. Teach the next generation *how* to think about FI rather than *what* to think.

A lot of parents want to leave money to their kids but are fearful it will be misused and spent frivolously. But what if you could give children money over time, money they don't have easy access to, and you could coach them to invest and grow it, and do this all in a tax-efficient manner?

Here are a couple of ideas for you to consider:

Strategic Cash Gifts

Rather than giving your kids "free" cash now, help your kids fund their retirement. Specifically, help them fund their tax-deferred accounts. In 2022, you can give away up to $16,000 to as many individuals—your kids, grandkids, their spouses—as you choose with no federal gift tax liability. A husband and wife can each make a $16,000 gift, meaning as a couple you could give each child (or any individual) up to $32,000 per year.[98]

To cultivate good habits, your "retirement" gifts could be based on some level of matching the child's contributions to their retirement accounts (e.g., 401[k], IRA, etc.). Many employers match employee contributions, so why not do effectively the same thing?

Consider the following common scenario. Your adult child can put up to $6,000 into an individual retirement account (IRA) (provided they have at least $6,000 of earned income) but is hesitant to do so. You could provide an incentive by offering to match their contribution at whatever rate you choose. For this example, you choose 50%. If your child contributes $200 per month, you would match that contribution with $100.

Giving small amounts over time can help you monitor their use (or misuse) of the funds. It will allow you to provide real-time coaching and guidance to your child—developing their FI knowledge base and sound financial habits while their portfolio is relatively small. The longer-term benefit (hopefully) is twofold: (1) they develop good financial habits early on; and (2) with your mentoring, your child will be in a much better position to manage an inheritance *if and when* it arrives.

Some might describe this as giving with strings attached. I view it as giving with wisdom attached. It can also help you avoid the unintended consequence of children counting on you for recurring cash "gifts" to cover some of their ongoing living expenses. If you constantly bail them out of a cash jam, they feel no downside pain to their overspending. Economists describe this type of bail-out as a "moral hazard." Do not empower your children to ignore the risks and consequences of poor cash management.

Donor-Advised Charitable Funds

Pass on your legacy of philanthropy. For a lot of families, it is a core family value that individual members give back to help their communities and, more broadly, society.

One tool some families use to support their philanthropic efforts is a donor-advised fund (DAF). Such a fund is a giving account established at a public charity. It allows you to make a charitable contribution, receive an immediate federal tax deduction, and then, over time, recommend specific charities to receive "grants" from the fund. (Several large money managers have public charities that sponsor this type of fund, including Fidelity, Vanguard, and Schwab, to name just a few. There are hundreds of smaller community foundations that also sponsor DAFs.)

In short, the fund sponsor invests your contributions and awaits your recommendations to distribute money to designated charitable organizations. Here is where legacy planning comes in. You can name a successor(s) for your account who will take over the responsibility (after you are gone) of granting funds to specific charities. In effect, you will have earmarked a piece of your heirs' "inheritance" to be used exclusively for charitable purposes.

> **NOTE:** As with any tax, estate, or financial planning ideas discussed in this book, you should consult with your tax and legal advisors before undertaking such endeavors.

Teach the next generation. Establish a methodical, reasoned approach to help your heirs avoid the sudden wealth syndrome.

And contemplate what author and finance professor Meir Statman often advocates: why not give money to the next generation with a warm hand rather than a cold one?[99]

PART TWO: INHERITING WEALTH

"Do what you can, with what you have, where you are."
—THEODORE ROOSEVELT

We often hear about so-called "trust fund kids" receiving large inheritances, but those "kids" are likely not kids at all. Most inheritances actually come later in life.

A 2016 study by Capital One found that only about 20% of households receive an inheritance (and that percentage has been relatively flat over the prior 30 years). The average age adults receive an inheritance is 51, with over 25% of inheritances going to adults over the age of 61.[100] That means that even *if* you inherit some wealth, it may not come until after you have lived two-thirds of your life! That's a whole lot of living to pay for on your own.

"I grew up with the priceless advantage of having to work for what I got."
—JACK BOGLE

As a potential heir, don't spend your time counting on other people's money (even that of your parents). The following line is quoted above and bears repeating here: *There is value in the struggle, lessons in failure, and character forged in the journey.* Find your own way in life.

A big inheritance can erase good financial habits. The windfall can encourage splurging on items and burning through cash (after all, it's "found money"). This can erode the long-term financial habits and discipline you are working so hard to achieve.

Relying on one's self to create long-term, lasting wealth is what this book is all about. Enjoying that wealth is the goal, which may or may not include receiving some amount of wealth as an inheritance.

Are your parents the ones who are quietly nervous about you squandering an inheritance? Show them you can handle an inheritance by demonstrating you don't need it. Have a life plan, be motivated and self-driven. Take an interest in personal finance. You don't need to be a financial whiz kid but you do need to show that you are motivated to learn, ambitious, and fully aware of the responsibilities that come with wealth. The more proficient you are with managing money, the more likely your parents will be comfortable giving you money to manage.

If and when an inheritance arrives, take a deep breath and immediately do nothing. Take the money and fold it into your overall FI plan. Patiently and deliberately evaluate the path forward. Then and only then, determine if there is any amount that can be reasonably allocated to current spending needs or wants, leaving the balance to continue to work toward your FI goals. As I have said before, understand the financial implications of the choices you make—preferably before you make them.

And if you do not receive an inheritance (the Capital One study suggests 80% of us will not), that's okay too. You have built your FI plan, charted your own life's course, and are well on your way to achieving FI and living life as a productive member of your community—and you did it your way!

A legacy of multigenerational wealth won't happen unless those in control of the purse strings, today and tomorrow, view their role as wealth stewards, not wealth spenders.

IN SUMMARY

Lessons for Wealth Creators

1. Give your heirs the most valuable financial gift you can: the wisdom to manage their own FI Portfolio, whether they will receive an inheritance or not.

2. If you choose to transfer some wealth, consider doing it in small doses (and tax-efficiently) over several years while you are around to teach and guide them on their FI journey.

3. Fly first class: your children are paying for it.

Lessons for Potential Heirs

1. Don't count on spending other people's money. View a potential inheritance as a privilege, not as a foregone conclusion or guarantee.

2. Any actual inherited money is a gift. Treat it as such. Don't let it burn a hole in your pocket. Add it to your FI Portfolio and let your FI plan guide how you invest and manage it.

3. More than anything else, find your own way in life.

SUGGESTIONS FOR ADDITIONAL READING

Tom McCullough and Keith Whitaker, *Wealth of Wisdom: The Top 50 Questions Wealthy Families Ask* (John Wiley & Sons, 2018).

Frazer Rice, *Wealth, Actually: Intelligent Decision-Making for the 1%* (Lioncrest Publishing, 2018).

17

GROWING YOUR WEALTH—THE CHECKLIST

"Be yourself. Everyone else is already taken."

—OSCAR WILDE

WE HAVE COVERED A LOT OF GROUND WHILE DISCUSSING SEVERAL pitfalls and hurdles as we contemplated how to chart our path to and through financial independence. So, I thought I would summarize key concepts in a short checklist for you—a quick reference tool whenever you need a refresher. Remember, it is the personalized planning process, not just a plan, that will lead you to your goals.

Take Inventory: (1) Get control of your income and expenditures. Understand all your sources of cash and where that cash is going. (2) Fully account for all assets that make up your FI Portfolio.

Planning: Use financial calculators to model out your Life's Complete Financial Arc: develop a robust and dynamic planning process that covers *both* the accumulation stage and the withdrawal stage. Purpose-built and goals-driven.

Save Monthly: Get started saving cash early and invest continuously. Let the power of compounding portfolio growth do the heavy lifting.

Skill vs. Luck: Recognize the difference and focus on what you can control. The amount of your monthly contributions and then monthly withdrawals are the two most important factors in your modeling, and both are completely within your control. Bull and bear markets are luck of the draw.

Investing: For the core of your FI Portfolio consider low-cost, broad-based index funds. (See the Appendix for specific recommendations.)

Speculating: Don't do it. But if you just can't resist the urge to have some "play money" in the stock market, keep it to no more than 10% of your FI Portfolio. And, good luck.

Course-Correct: Periodically review progress and make needed changes focusing on what you can control: contributions, withdrawals, realistic goals, investment selection, and following a dynamic planning process.

Block Out Noise: Don't chase the hot hand, the hot stock, the hot story. Stay calm and remain cool. Have faith in your planning process.

Seek Out Wisdom: Read, learn, discuss with those you trust. Develop your own informed perspective and do not forget the lessons history has taught us.

Enjoy the Journey: Life is not a dress rehearsal: there is no do-over. Get up and dance.

18

EPILOGUE

"Plans are worthless but planning is everything."

—DWIGHT D. EISENHOWER

THERE ARE A LOT OF REASONS FOR PLANNING OUT YOUR FI JOURNEY, but none greater than the opportunity to acquire the most valuable asset on this planet—freedom. Freedom to choose to live your life on your terms. Money won't buy happiness. But an FI Portfolio, nurtured properly, will allow you the *opportunity* to explore what happiness means for you and those with whom you choose to share your time, energy, and love. Pursue (today and tomorrow) those interests that bring you the most joy, meaning, and fulfillment.

As with most things in life, the more you plan for FI, including course-correcting along the way, the less time you will need to worry about the outcome.

And less time spent worrying about the future means more time spent enjoying the present—living your best life now, with the satisfaction and comfort of knowing your financial future is in good hands...your own two hands.

Over your Life's Complete Financial Arc, assumptions, projections, and goals will undoubtedly change and evolve. Your dynamic planning process is the one constant that will hold it all together.

PCR: Plan, Course-Correct, Repeat.

Appendix

CORE PORTFOLIO SUGGESTIONS FOR YOUR CONSIDERATION

FOR LONG-TERM INVESTMENT SELECTION, CONSIDER STARTING YOUR research with these low-cost, broad-based index funds (all of which currently have expense ratios under 0.1%):

Fund Name:	Ticker:
EQUITIES (US):	
Vanguard Total Stock Market Index ETF	VTI
Schwab Total Stock Market Index Mutual Fund	SWTSX
Fidelity ZERO Total Market Index Mutual Fund	FZROX
Vanguard S&P 500 ETF	VOO
SPDR Portfolio S&P 500 ETF	SPLG

Fund Name:	Ticker:
EQUITIES (NON–US):	
Vanguard Total Int'l Stock ETF	VXUS
iShares Core MSCI Total Int'l Stock ETF	IXUS
BONDS (US):	
Vanguard Total Bond Market ETF	BND
iShares Core Total USD Bond Market ETF	IUSB
BONDS (NON–US):	
Vanguard Total Int'l Bond ETF	BNDX
iShares Core Int'l Aggregate Bond ETF	IAGG

BIBLIOGRAPHY

Bavaria, Steven. *The Income Factory: An Investor's Guide to Consistent Lifetime Returns*. New York: McGraw Hill Education, 2020.

Bernstein, William J. *The Delusions of Crowds: Why People Go Mad in Groups*. New York: Grove/Atlantic, 2021.

Bodie, Zvi and Rachelle Taqqu. *Risk Less and Prosper: Your Guide to Safer Investing*. Hoboken: John Wiley & Sons, 2012.

Bogle, John C. *The Clash of the Cultures: Investment vs. Speculation*. Hoboken: John Wiley & Sons, 2012.

Bogle, John C. *Enough: True Measures of Money, Business, and Life*. Hoboken: John Wiley & Sons, 2009.

Bogle, John C. *The Little Book of Common Sense Investing: The Only Way to Guarantee Your Fair Share of Stock Market Returns*. Hoboken: John Wiley & Sons, 2017.

Carlson, Ben. *A Wealth of Common Sense: Why Simplicity Trumps Complexity in Any Investment Plan*. Hoboken: John Wiley & Sons, 2015.

Carlson, Ben. *Don't Fall For It: A Short History of Financial Scams*. John Wiley & Sons, Inc., 2020.

Carlson, Robert C. *The New Rules of Retirement: Strategies for a Secure Future*. Hoboken: John Wiley & Sons, 2016.

Collins, J. L. *The Simple Path to Wealth: Your Road Map to Financial Independence and a Rich, Free Life.* CreateSpace Publishing, 2016.

Duke, Annie. *Thinking in Bets: Making Smarter Decisions When You Don't Have All the Facts.* New York: Penguin Publishing Group, 2018.

Ellis, Charles D. *Winning the Loser's Game: Timeless Strategies for Successful Investing.* New York: McGraw Hill Education, 2017.

Goldfarb, Brent and David A. Kirsch. *Bubbles and Crashes: The Boom and Bust of Technological Innovation.* Stanford: Stanford University Press, 2019.

Goldie, Daniel C. and Gordon S. Murray. *The Investment Answer.* New York: Business Plus, 2011.

Graham, Benjamin. *The Intelligent Investor: The Definitive Book on Value Investing* with commentary by Jason Zweig. New York: HarperCollins, 2003.

Green, William. *Richer, Wiser, Happier: How the World's Greatest Investors Win in Markets and Life.* New York: Scribner, 2021.

Housel, Morgan. *The Psychology of Money: Timeless Lessons on Wealth, Greed, and Happiness.* Petersfield: Harriman House Ltd., 2020.

Katusa, Marin. *The Rise of America: Remaking the World Order.* Katusa Research Publishing, 2021.

Kirkpatrick, Darrow. *Can I Retire Yet?: How to Make the Biggest Financial Decision of the Rest of Your Life.* Chattanooga: StructureByDesign, 2016.

Kiyosaki, Robert T. *Rich Dad Poor Dad: What the Rich Teach Their Kids about Money—That the Poor and Middle Class Do Not!* New York: Warner Books, 1998.

Klarman, Seth A. *Margin of Safety: Risk-Averse Value Investing Strategies for the Thoughtful Investor.* New York: HarperCollins, 1991.

Lefevre, Edwin. *Reminiscences of a Stock Operator.* Garden City: George H. Doran Company, 1923.

Lewis, Michael. *The Big Short: Inside the Doomsday Machine.* New York: W.W. Norton & Company, 2010.

Lynch, Peter. *One Up on Wall Street.* New York: Fireside, 1989.

Malkiel, Burton G. *A Random Walk Down Wall Street: The Time-Tested Strategy for Successful Investing*. New York: W.W. Norton & Company, 2019.

Malkiel, Burton G. and Charles D. Ellis. *The Elements of Investing: Easy Lessons for Every Investor*. Hoboken: John Wiley & Sons, 2021.

Mallouk, Peter and Tony Robbins. *The Path: Accelerating Your Journey to Financial Freedom*. New York: Post Hill Press, 2020.

Mamula, Chris, Brad Barrett, and Jonathan Mendonsa. *Choose FI: Your Blueprint to Financial Independence*. Glen Allen: Choose FI Media, 2019.

Marks, Howard. *Mastering the Market Cycle: Getting the Odds on Your Side*. Boston: Houghton Mifflin Harcourt, 2018.

Marks, Howard. *The Most Important Thing Illuminated: Uncommon Sense for the Thoughtful Investor*. New York: Columbia University Press, 2013.

Mauboussin, Michael J. *The Success Equation: Untangling Skill and Luck in Business, Sports, and Investing*. Boston: Harvard Business Review Press, 2012.

McCullough, Tom and Keith Whitaker. *Wealth of Wisdom: The Top 50 Questions Wealthy Families Ask*. Chichester: John Wiley & Sons, 2018.

Moss, Wes. *You Can Retire Sooner Than You Think: The 5 Money Secrets of the Happiest Retirees*. New York: McGraw Hill Education, 2014.

Murray, Nick. *Simple Wealth, Inevitable Wealth*. The Nick Murray Company, 2019.

Pfau, Wade. *How Much Can I Spend in Retirement?: A Guide to Investment-Based Retirement Income Strategies*. McLean: Retirement Researcher Media, 2017.

Pfau, Wade. *Safety-First Retirement Planning: An Integrated Approach for a Worry-Free Retirement*. Vienna: Retirement Researcher Media, 2019.

Portnoy, Brian. *The Geometry of Wealth: How to Shape a Life of Money and Meaning*. Petersfield: Harriman House, 2018.

Quinn, Jane Bryant. *How to Make Your Money Last: The Indispensable Retirement Guide*. New York: Simon & Schuster, 2016.

Rice, Frazer. *Wealth, Actually: Intelligent Decision-Making for the 1%*. Lioncrest Publishing, 2018.

Richards, Carl. *The Behavior Gap: Simple Ways to Stop Doing Dumb Things with Money*. New York: Penguin Publishing Group, 2012.

Richards, Carl. *The One-Page Financial Plan: A Simple Way to Be Smart About Your Money*. New York: Penguin Publishing Group, 2015.

Robin, Vicki and Joe Dominguez. *Your Money or Your Life: 9 Steps to Transforming Your Relationship with Money and Achieving Financial Independence*. New York: Penguin Publishing Group, 2008.

Rosling, Hans. *Factfulness: Ten Reasons We're Wrong About the World—and Why Things Are Better Than You Think*. New York: Flatiron Books, 2018.

Sabatier, Grant. *Financial Freedom: A Proven Path to All the Money You Will Ever Need*. New York: Penguin Publishing Group, 2019.

Schroeder, Alice. *The Snowball: Warren Buffett and the Business of Life*. New York: Bantam Books, 2009.

Schultheis, Bill. *The Coffeehouse Investor's Ground Rules: Save, Invest, and Plan for a Life of Wealth and Happiness*. Hoboken: John Wiley & Sons, 2021.

Schwed, Fred. *Where Are the Customers' Yachts? or A Good Hard Look at Wall Street*. Hoboken: John Wiley & Sons, 2006.

Sethi, Rami. *I Will Teach You to Be Rich*. New York: Workman Publishing Co., 2019.

Siegel, Jeremy J. *Stocks for the Long Run: The Definitive Guide to Financial Market Returns and Long-Term Investment Strategies*. New York: McGraw Hill Education, 2014.

Stanley, Thomas J., and William D. Danko. *The Millionaire Next Door: The Surprising Secrets of America's Wealthy*. Marietta: Longstreet Press, 1996.

Stein, J. David. *Money for the Rest of Us: 10 Questions to Master Successful Investing*. New York: McGraw Hill Education, 2020.

Taleb, Nassim Nicholas. *Fooled by Randomness: The Hidden Role of Chance in Life and in the Markets*. New York: Random House, 2004.

Thaler, Richard H. *Misbehaving: The Making of Behavioral Economics*. New York: W.W. Norton & Company, 2015.

Tresidder, Todd. *How Much Money Do I Need to Retire? Uncommon Financial Planning Wisdom for a Stress-Free Retirement.* FinancialMentor, 2020.

Welch, Suzy. *10-10-10: 10 Minutes, 10 Months, 10 Years: A Life Transforming Idea.* New York: Simon & Schuster, 2009.

Zweig, Jason. *Your Money and Your Brain: How the New Science of Neuroeconomics Can Help Make You Rich.* New York: Simon & Schuster, 2007.

ENDNOTES

1 Throughout this book, the term "FI Portfolio" is used to reference the total of all your investment accounts and income-producing assets that are earmarked for long-term (i.e., retirement) financial planning, including, but not limited to: employer-sponsored retirement accounts such as 401(k) or 403(b) plans; individual retirement accounts (Roth or traditional IRA); taxable brokerage accounts, savings accounts, stocks, bonds, rental real estate, annuities, etc.

2 *The Gambler*, directed by Rupert Wyatt, written by William Monahan, featuring Mark Wahlberg and John Goodman (2014, Paramount Pictures), WAusJackBauer, "The Gambler—Fuck You," YouTube Video, 4:29, February 5, 2016, https://www.youtube.com/watch?v=y6yCmdIkw_E.

3 "Retirement Planning Calculator with Investment and Withdrawal Schedule," financial-calculators.com, June 19, 2021, https://financial-calculators.com/retirement-calculator.

4 "Retirement Nest Egg Calculator," Vanguard.com, June 19, 2021, https://retirementplans.vanguard.com/VGApp/pe/pubeducation/calculators/RetirementNestEggCalc.jsf.

5 "Compound Interest Is Man's Greatest Invention," QuoteInvestigator.com, October 31, 2011, https://quoteinvestigator.com/2011/10/31/compound-interest.

6 Paraphrasing an apocryphal quote attributed to Albert Einstein. The full quote: "Compound interest is the eighth wonder of the world. He who understands it, earns it; he who doesn't, pays it."

7   Steven F. Venti and David A. Wise, "Choice, Chance, and Wealth Dispersion at Retirement," National Bureau of Economic Research (February 2000), https://www.nber.org/papers/w7521.

8   Morgan Housel, *The Psychology of Money* (Petersfield: Harriman House, 2020): 53.

9   John C. Bogle, *Enough: True Measures of Money, Business, and Life* (Hoboken: Wiley, 2009): 66–67.

10   William F. Sharpe, "Likely Gains from Market Timing," *Financial Analysts Journal* 31, no. 2 (March/April 1975): 60–69.

11   David Kelly, "Guide to the Markets, US|2Q 2021|As of March 31, 2021," JP Morgan, accessed June 15, 2021, https://am.jpmorgan.com/us/en/asset-management/adv/insights/market-insights/guide-to-the-markets. Note: this website is updated quarterly.

12   Ibid.

13   Jackie Wattles, "Warren Buffett Beat the Hedge Funds. Here's How," CNN, February 24, 2018, https://money.cnn.com/2018/02/24/investing/warren-buffett-annual-letter-hedge-fund-bet/index.html.

14   Berlinda Liu and Gaurav Sinha, "SPIVA US Scorecard," S&P Dow Jones, accessed June 15, 2021, https://www.spglobal.com/spdji/en/documents/spiva/spiva-us-year-end-2020.pdf.

15   Ibid.

16   Berlinda Liu and Gaurav Sinha, "US Persistence Scorecard," S&P Dow Jones, accessed June 15, 2021, https://www.spglobal.com/spdji/en/documents/spiva/persistence-scorecard-year-end-2020.pdf.

17   Hendrik Bessembinder, "Do Stocks Outperform Treasury Bills?" *Journal of Financial Economics* 129, no. 3 (May 28, 2018): 440–57.

18   Eugene Kim, "Jeff Bezos to Employees: 'One Day, Amazon Will Fail' but Our Job Is to Delay It as Long as Possible," CNBC, November 15, 2018, https://www.cnbc.com/2018/11/15/bezos-tells-employees-one-day-amazon-will-fail-and-to-stay-hungry.html.

19   Craig Lazzara, "The Skew Is Not New," S&P Dow Jones, February 22, 2018, https://www.indexologyblog.com/2018/02/22/the-skew-is-not-new.

20   Eugene F. Fama and Kenneth R. French, "Luck versus Skill in the Cross-Section of Mutual Fund Returns," *Journal of Finance* LXV, no. 5 (September 21, 2010): 1915–47. If you'd like to go deeper on this topic, this study provides an in-depth scholarly analysis on the index vs. active debate among mutual funds.

21 Francis M. Kinniry Jr., "Putting a Value on Your Value: Quantifying Vanguard Advisor's Alpha," Vanguard.com, February 2019, https://www.vanguard.com/pdf/ISGQVAA.pdf.

22 Charles D. Ellis, *Winning the Loser's Game: Timeless Strategies for Successful Investing* (New York City: McGraw Hill, 2017): Chapter 21.

23 "Consumer Guide to Choosing a Financial Professional," University of Illinois Extension, accessed June 15, 2021, https://web.extension.illinois.edu/financialpro/consumer.cfm.

24 Carl Richards (@behaviorgap), Twitter, May 24, 2013.

25 Howard Marks, *The Most Important Thing Illuminated: Uncommon Sense for the Thoughtful Investor* (New York City: Columbia University Press, 2013): 4.

26 John C. Bogle, *The Clash of the Cultures: Investment vs. Speculation.* (Hoboken: John Wiley & Sons, 2012): 5.

27 Adriana De La Cruz, Alejandra Medina, and Yung Tang, "Owners of the World's Listed Companies," OECD Capital Market Series, Paris, 2019, https://www.oecd.org/corporate/Owners-of-the-Worlds-Listed-Companies.htm.

28 Ibid.

29 "ETFGI Reports Assets in the Global ETFs and ETPs Industry which Will Turn 30 Years Old in March Started the New Decade with a Record 6.35 Trillion US Dollars," ETFGI.com. January 16, 2020, https://etfgi.com/news/press-releases/2020/01/etfgi-reports-assets-global-etfs-and-etps-industry-which-will-turn-30.

30 "Fiscal Year 2020 Annual Report," CFA Institute, 2020, https://www.cfainstitute.org/-/media/documents/corporate-record/annual-report-2020.ashx.

31 "FPSB Affiliate Organizations," FPSB, March 26, 2021, https://www.fpsb.org/about/member-organizations.

32 Michael J. Mauboussin, *The Success Equation: Untangling Skill and Luck in Business, Sports, and Investing* (Cambridge: Harvard Business Review Press, 2012): 53.

33 Nick Farriella, "This Side of Paradise: A Letter from F. Scott Fitzgerald, Quarantined in the South of France," McSweeney's Quarterly Subscriptions, March 13, 2020, https://www.mcsweeneys.net/articles/this-side-of-paradise-a-letter-from-f-scott-fitzgerald-quarantined-in-the-south-of-france.

34 Matthew J. Bruccoli, editor, *F. Scott Fitzgerald: A Life in Letters* (New York City: Scribner, 1994).

35   The Buffett numbers in the preceding two paragraphs are the author's rough estimates based on publicly available information.

36   Howard Marks, "Expert Opinion," Oaktree Capital, 2017, https://www. oaktreecapital.com/docs/default-source/memos/expert-opinion.pdf.

37   Plaza Staff, "Man Wins $270k at the Plaza after Betting His Life Savings," PlazaHotelCasino.com, February 12, 2019, https://www.plazahotelcasino.com/ blog/man-wins-270k-plaza.

38   Leverage Academy, "Fantastic Michael Burry UCLA Commencement Speech on US & European Financial Crises," *Business Insider*, June 24, 2012, https://www.businessinsider.com/fantastic-michael-burry-ucla-commence-ment-speech-on-us-and-european-financial-crises-2012-6.

39   Michael Burry's story was immortalized in the 2010 book *The Big Short* by Michael Lewis, which was also the basis for the 2015 film of the same name.

40   Mary Schmich, "Advice, Like Youth, Probably Just Wasted on the Young," *Chicago Tribune*, June 1, 1997, https://www.chicagotribune.com/columns/ chi-schmich-sunscreen-column-column.html.

41   Ocelotl Co, "Everybody's Free to Wear Sunscreen—Baz Luhrmann," YouTube Video, 7:12, August 29, 2016, https://www.youtube.com/watch?v=Zx-EHGAY7LbY.

42   Nobel Prize winners: Robert Fogel (1993), George Akerlof (2001), Daniel Kahneman (2002), Elinor Ostrom (2009), Robert Shiller (2013), and Richard Thaler (2017).

43   Jason Zweig, *Your Money and Your Brain: How the New Science of Neuroeconomics Can Help Make You Rich* (Delran: Simon & Schuster, 2007): 6.

44   "2020 QAIB Report," Dalbar, December 31, 2019, https://wealthwatchad-visors.com/wp-content/uploads/2020/03/QAIB_PremiumEdition2020_WWA. pdf.

45   Suzy Welch, *10-10-10: 10 Minutes, 10 Months, 10 Years: A Life-Transforming Idea* (Delran: Simon & Schuster, 2019).

46   Julie Creswell, "Speedy New Traders Make Waves Far from Wall St.," *The New York Times*, May 16, 2010, https://www.nytimes.com/2010/05/17/busi-ness/17trade.html.

47   "20th Annual Transamerica Retirement Survey," Transamerica Center for Retirement Studies, December 2020, https://transamericacenter.org/retire-ment-research/20th-annual-retirement-survey.

48 "Retirement Confidence Survey Summary Report," Employee Benefit Research Institute, April 23, 2020, https://www.ebri.org/docs/default-source/rcs/2020-rcs/2020-rcs-summary-report.pdf?sfvrsn=84bc3d2f_7.

49 Don A. Moore et al., "Positive Illusions and Forecasting Errors in Mutual Fund Investment Decisions," *Organizational Behavior and Human Decision Processes* 79, no. 2 (August 1999): 95–114.

50 Kent Daniel and David Hirshleifer, "Overconfident Investors, Predictable Returns, and Excessive Trading," *Journal of Economic Perspectives* 29, no. 4 (Fall 2015): 61–88, https://www.aeaweb.org/articles?id=10.1257/jep.29.4.61.

51 Benjamin Graham, *The Intelligent Investor: The Definitive Book on Value Investing* with commentary by Jason Zweig (New York City: HarperCollins, 2003): 18.

52 Ibid., 21.

53 Seth A. Klarman, *Margin of Safety: Risk-Averse Value Investing Strategies for the Thoughtful Investor* (New York City: HarperCollins, 1991): 3–4.

54 Saikat Chatterjee and Thyagaraju Adinarayan, "Buy, Sell, Repeat! No Room for 'Hold' in Whipsawing Markets," *Reuters*, August 3, 2020, https://www.reuters.com/article/us-health-coronavirus-short-termism-anal/buy-sell-repeat-no-room-for-hold-in-whipsawing-markets-idUSKBN24Z0XZ.

55 Stefan Sharkansky, "Mutual Fund Performance and the Consequences of Fees, Trading Costs and Taxes," Personal Fund, December 12, 2019, https://personalfund.com/Mutual%20Fund%20Performance%20and%20Costs%20v2%20FINAL%202019-12-12.pdf.

56 "Tulip Mania," Wikipedia.org, accessed June 19, 2021, https://en.wikipedia.org/wiki/Tulip_mania.

57 Josh Katz, "Who Will Be President?" *The New York Times*, November 8, 2016, https://www.nytimes.com/interactive/2016/upshot/presidential-polls-forecast.html.

58 Annie Duke, *Thinking in Bets: Making Smarter Decisions When You Don't Have All the Facts* (Westminster: Penguin Publishing Group, 2018): 34.

59 S. Patrick Viguerie, Ned Calder, Brian Hindo, "2021 Corporate Longevity Forecast," Innosight.com, May 2021, https://www.innosight.com/insight/creative-destruction.

60 Burton G. Malkiel, *A Random Walk Down Wall Street: The Time-Tested Strategy for Successful Investing* (New York City: W.W. Norton & Company, 2019).

61 "Bubbles: From 'Tronics' to 'Dot com,'" *Forbes*, January 14, 1999, https://www.forbes.com/1999/01/14/mu3.html?sh=30b3a66a4aea#5b3a-2faa4aea1/4Bubbles.

62 Malkiel, *A Random Walk Down Wall Street*, 57.

63 Michael J. Cooper, Orlin Dimitrov, and P. Raghavendra Rau, "A Rose.com by Any Other Name," *The Journal of Finance* LVI, no. 6 (December 2001): 2371–88, doi.org/10.2139/ssrn.242376.

64 Michael J. Cooper et al., "Managerial Actions in Response to a Market Downturn: Valuation Effects of Name Changes in the Dot.com Decline," *Journal of Corporate Finance* 11, nos. 1–2 (April 2004): 319–55, http://home.business.utah.edu/finmc/Dotcom_Paper_JCFVersion_050305.pdf.

65 Rupert Neate, "Tiny US Soft Drinks Firm Changes Name to Cash in on Bitcoin Mania," *The Guardian*, December 21, 2017, https://www.theguardian.com/technology/2017/dec/21/us-soft-drinks-firm-changes-name-bitcoin-long-island-iced-tea-corp-shares-blockchain.

66 Lisa Pham, "This Company Added the Word 'Blockchain' to Its Name and Saw Its Shares Surge 394%," Bloomberg, October 27, 2017, https://www.bloomberg.com/news/articles/2017-10-27/what-s-in-a-name-u-k-stock-surges-394-on-blockchain-rebrand.

67 John Detrixhe and Justin Rohrlich, "The FBI Thinks Long Island Iced Tea's Infamous Pivot to Blockchain was Sweetened by Insider Trading." Quartz, July 25, 2019, https://qz.com/1659246/the-fbi-wants-more-information-about-long-blockchain.

68 Anise C. Wallace, "Why This Market Cycle Isn't Different," *The New York Times*, October 11, 1987, https://www.nytimes.com/1987/10/11/business/investing-why-this-market-cycle-isnt-different.html.

69 John Bilton, "Long-Term Capital Market Assumptions," JPMorgan, accessed October 19, 2020, https://am.jpmorgan.com/us/en/asset-management/institutional/insights/portfolio-insights/ltcma.

70 Molly Mercer, Alan R. Palmiter, and Ahmed E. Taha, "Worthless Warnings? Testing the Effectiveness of Disclaimers in Mutual Fund Advertisements," *Journal of Empirical Legal Studies* 7, no. 3 (April 8, 2010): 429–59.

71 Barry P. Barbash, "Remembering the Past: Mutual Funds and the Lessons of the Wonder Years," SEC.gov., December 4, 1997, https://www.sec.gov/news/speech/speecharchive/1997/spch199.txt.

72   Sarah McVeigh, "What It's Like to Grow Up with More Money Than You'll Ever Spend," *The Cut*, March 28, 2019, https://www.thecut.com/2019/03/abigail-disney-has-more-money-than-shell-ever-spend.html.

73   Benjamin Kline Hunnicutt, "The End of Shorter Hours," *Labor History* 25, no. 3 (1984): 373–404, DOI: 10.1080/00236568408584762.

74   Ibid.

75   Ibid.

76   Ibid.

77   National Archives (n.d.), *Congress Establishes Thanksgiving*, https://www.archives.gov/legislative/features/thanksgiving.

78   Bob Sutton, "'The Knowledge that I Have Got Enough' Kurt Vonnegut, Joe Heller, and a Thanksgiving Message," *Medium*, November 23, 2016, https://medium.com/@bobsutton/kurt-vonnegut-joe-heller-and-a-thanksgiving-message-8a31ca397888.

79   Although it is often attributed to Jefferson, according to at least one source, Monticello.org, this quotation has not been found in any of the writings of Thomas Jefferson.

80   Peter L. Bernstein, *Against the Gods: The Remarkable Story of Risk* (Hoboken: John Wiley & Sons, 1998): 261.

81   Nir Kaissar, "Dividend Cuts Shouldn't Worry Investors: A Look at How Other Recent Downturns Played Out Suggests the Fears about Dividends Are Overdone," *Investment News*, April 8, 2020, https://www.investmentnews.com/dividend-cuts-shouldnt-worry-investors-191207.

82   "The Market Can Remain Irrational Longer than You Can Remain Solvent," Quote Investigator, August 9, 2011, https://quoteinvestigator.com/2011/08/09/remain-solvent. This aphorism is often attributed to John Maynard Keynes, but it appears likely that it originated with A. Gary Shilling in the 1980s.

83   "S&P 500 Total Returns," SlickCharts.com (n.d.), July 12, 2021, https://www.slickcharts.com/sp500/returns.

84   William J. Bernstein, *The Four Pillars of Investing: Lessons for Building a Winning Portfolio* (New York City: McGraw-Hill, 2010): 229–41.

85   Darrow Kirkpatrick, *Can I Retire Yet? How to Make the Biggest Financial Decision of the Rest of Your Life* (StructureByDesign, 2016): 200.

86   Ibid, 201.

87   Chris Brooks et al., "The Importance of Staying Positive: The Impact of Emotions on Attitude to Risk," SSRN, May 12, 2020, https://papers.ssrn.com/sol3/papers.cfm?abstract_id=3579303.

88   Ibid.

89   Jason Zweig, "What Harry Markowitz Meant," JasonZweig.com, October 2, 2017, https://jasonzweig.com/?s=Harry+Markowitz.

90   Fidelity Viewpoints, "How Can I Make My Retirement Savings Last?" Fidelity, August 19, 2021, https://www.fidelity.com/viewpoints/retirement/how-long-will-savings-last.

91   Wade Pfau, "How Much of Your Savings Can You Spend Each Year in Retirement? The Answer," Forbes, January 10, 2018, https://www.forbes.com/sites/wadepfau/2018/01/10/william-bengens-safemax-updated-to-2018/?sh=7a3884b46be4.

92   Brett Arends, "The Inventor of the '4% Rule' Just Changed It," Market Watch, October 22, 2020, https://www.marketwatch.com/story/the-inventor-of-the-4-rule-just-changed-it-11603380557.

93   "The Great Wealth Transfer," Cerulli Associates, accessed June 19, 2021, https://info.cerulli.com/HNW-Transfer-of-Wealth-Cerulli.html.

94   Chris Taylor, "70% of Rich Families Lose Their Wealth by the Second Generation," Money, June 17, 2015, https://money.com/rich-families-lose-wealth.

95   Missy Sullivan, "Lost Inheritance," The Wall Street Journal, March 8, 2013, https://www.wsj.com/articles/SB10001424127887324662404578334663271139552.

96   Pablo S. Torre, "How (and Why) Athletes Go Broke," Sports Illustrated, March 23, 2009, https://vault.si.com/vault/2009/03/23/how-and-why-athletes-go-broke.

97   Jill Shipley quoted in Tom McCullough and Keith Whitaker, Wealth of Wisdom: The Top 50 Questions Wealthy Families Ask (Hoboken: John Wiley & Sons, 2018): 146.

98   In late 2021, US President Joe Biden is proposing tax law changes that could impact gifting rules. Consult your tax advisor.

99   Meir Statman quoted in McCullough and Whitaker, Wealth of Wisdom, 59.

100 Matt Fellowes and Lincoln Plews, How Inheritances Help Households Afford Retirement, Capital One, November 19, 2019, retrieved on June 19, 2021.